ATROPOS PRESS
new york • dresden

© 2013 by Alain Badiou
Think Media EGS Series is supported by the European Graduate School

ATROPOS PRESS
New York • Dresden

151 First Avenue # 14, New York, N.Y. 10003

cover design: Peggy Bloomer
cover photo: Sierra Bloomer
all rights reserved

978-0-9885170-2-8

The Subject
of
Change

Author's Note About this Text

"Ce texte provient de notes prises par Duane Rousselle lors de mon séminaire de l'été 2012 à l'European Graduate School. C'est donc le reflet d'une exposition orale, souvent improvisée, et qui ne correspond à aucun texte écrit existant. Je n'ai pas relu ces notes, car j'aurais eu envie de tout réécrire, ce qui n'était pas dans l'esprit de cette tentative. Par conséquent, tout usage et toute citation de ce texte devra être accompagnée d'une indication précise de sa provenance, de façon à ce que personne ne puisse penser que je l'ai écrit ou revu." — *Alain Badiou*

"This text is based on notes taken by Duane Rousselle during the seminar I presented at the European Graduate School in the summer of 2012. It, then, reflects an oral contribution, with some degree of improvisation, and does not correspond to any written text. I did not re-read those notes as this would have lead me to a complete rewriting, which would not have been consistent with the initial spirit of this seminar. Consequently, any use or quotation of this text will have to be accompanied with a precise indication of its origin, so that nobody could think that I have either written or proof-read it."
— *Alain Badiou, translated by Isabelle Vodoz*

Editor's Preface

In his book *Conditions* – a book that only reached the English speaking world seventeen years after its original French publication – Alain Badiou claimed that there are three essential functions of the institution of philosophy: an address, a transmission, and an inscription. Relatedly, an institution of philosophy must be capable of organizing the possibility for a *poste restante,* a *maison de passe,* and an underground printing press. The importance of this task resides in the crucial work of printing, editing, and distributing synopses, notes, and books through the laborious conviction of disciples and custodians.

Badiou occupies the place of the teacher whose primary responsibility rests on the transmission of tradition. The transmission occurs as a consequence of the teacher, the master, the professor, or, as it happens, the old man. Clearly, Badiou occupies all of these roles. However, what concerns us today is that he is an old man and that the old man is the man who is approaching death. In fact, he does not shy away from this designation. Rather, he acknowledges this point with a smile: "Do not say that I am really a young man because it is not true. I know that I am seventy-five years old." Our teacher is fully aware that he is at the "beginning of the last straight line of life." The possibility of the death of the old man necessitates a thinking about the preservation of the transmission of the future. Finally, the possibility of a transmission from the old man in the future requires, at minimum, an address, some disciples, and a transcript. And so we return to the point that an institution of philosophy requires an address, a transmission, and an inscription, and that these three functions are best served by the *poste restante,* the *maison de passe,* and the underground printing press.

Perhaps the old man is only truly involved in the address. In this case, we must approach the question of the possibility of an audience. The question of the audience relates fundamentally to the question of the existence of the reader. For you, the reader of this text, as for the students in the classroom with Badiou in Saas-Fee, Switzerland, the audience is something like a generic set. All of you, as a set of readers, are not collectively identified according to any precise property. Consequently, the teacher can not presume the underlying motivations of the student or reader. His transmission must be something like a void address. Precisely, philosophy transmits itself through the void of its address insofar as there is an audience or readership whom are a generic set and who decide, very often against all evidence, that the teaching or the book is addressed to them. In some sense, the book you have in your hands is not transmitted to the public. It is distributed underground and to disciples. We are, against all evidence, disciples of the change provoked by its transmission.

The *poste restante* involves a transmission which is a void address to a generic set. In the context of the readership, like the context of the classroom we shared in Saas-Fee, Badiou claims that "it is not because you are all the same that you are here." Rather, we all come to the text and to the classroom with different motivations and different trajectories. This is what constitutes our genericity as a set of readers or students of the teachings. Badiou has put this rather nice: "there is no constant property which defines your presence here [...] and so, you are a generic set. If you are a generic set, how is it that I can suppose that the question of change is the same question for all of you?" In fact, we can not suppose a property though which the readership is united in their desire to answer the question of change. Rather, we suppose a multiplicity of motivations and a multiplicity of worlds within which the book will be reader. Already we are approaching the question of being in relation to a world. Within the language of the mathematics of set theory we know being is multiplicity. However, being is always localized within a world and subject to the order of the world.

The Subject of Change is a sustained engagement with the concept of change. However, it is also the product of a change. It is the transition of an editor into a disciple through the transmission of a void address. You should know that I initially approached Badiou's teachings with caution. I was, and remain, a student of Slavoj Zizek because I was, and remain, a student of Jacques Lacan. Moreover, I was, and remain, an anarchist. Something in the seminars provoked a profound change in me. For example, the system of thinking that Badiou constructed in the classroom provoked new ways of thinking about problems that have long plagued the anarchist tradition. Yet, I note with interest, his system of thought was not necessarily opposed to what today goes by the name post-anarchism or the new anarchism. This was not a solitary change, I noticed students and professors engaged in prolonged debates outside of the classroom and in the coffee shops and bars of Saas-Fee. We were all changed in different ways by the teaching. It became increasingly obvious that something unsayable had been introduced into my own experience and that this was absolutely different from what was introduced into the experience of other students and professors. Paradoxically, something about it was also the same. Badiou's discourse cut across our differences as students of his address. If I may be so bold, I believe that it was with the courage to work through the anxiety that Badiou's system provoked in me that I discovered the opportunity to organize these teachings into an edited book for anybody to read.

I would like to thank Wolfgang Schirmacher, program director at the European Graduate School, for permitting me to transcribe and edit this manuscript for Atropos Press. In a school unlike any other, Wolfgang has allowed Badiou's seminars to be read by anybody. In this respect, Wolfgang occupies that integral position of the custodian of the institution of philosophy. As Badiou has put it in *Conditions*: "custodians of the institution [are] those that constitute its core [...] they have care and concern for its 'holding together'; [...] they themselves are cognizant of the paradoxical connections of the address and transmission, of inscription and the address, and of inscription and transmission." It is with the support of Wolfgang, Badiou, and Atropos Press that I can envision the *maison de passe* in the inauguration of what may be the publication of the first seminar series of Alain Badiou – the translation of a conviction that seminar attendance must be open to all.

In this respect, I am grateful to Atropos Press for agreeing to publish the manuscript before having it in their hands. Atropos Press is the small independent and somewhat underground publishing company of the European Graduate School. They have had the audacity to circulate texts that do not necessarily do well on the market. Our publisher has put this very well: "the unexpected lay in the discovery that the numbers did not matter [...] what mattered was that the books were in circulation." I am convinced that this book *will* matter. Moreover, I am thoroughly convinced that Atropos fulfils the function of the underground printing press. It is my hope that this manuscript will inaugurate an entire series of manuscripts – one for each consecutive year – of carefully edited transcriptions of the seminars of one of the greatest philosophers to have ever lived. My promise is that I will continue to try my best to organize the possibility for this to continue to occur.

I would like to thank the two anonymous students at the European Graduate School for looking over the edited draft of their respective questions and for pointing out areas of improvement. Finally, I would like to thank Alain Badiou for his generosity, teachings, and time. Let us hope that this book provokes something in you, as it did for me.

Duane Rousselle
November, 2012

The Subject of Change

Lessons from the European Graduate School, 2012

By Alain Badiou

Edited by Duane Rousselle

Contents

Day One

Seminar One
*The Question of Change * Teachings of an Old Man * The Transmission of Tradition*
*Organizing the Youth * Repetition and Profound Ecology * A Modern Tradition*
*A Peace Treaty with History and Nature * A Non-Religious Vision of Death*
*Two Versions of Change * A New Philosophical Tradition*

Our question during this session will be the question of change. It will be our most important question. What is a change? What is a true change? What is a false change? Is change better than immobility? What are the different types of change? What is a change in society? What is a political change? What is a change in (sensible) forms? What is a change in art? What is a change in knowledge? For example, what is a scientific change? What is a change in life? And what is a change in private life?

More generally, we can examine the general conditions of a change or the context of a change. In fact, it is a question about whether or not a change is always localized in a specific place. There is also the question of the possibility of global or total change. This is also a valid question. And so we also have the question of what we can name the place of a change, the localization of a change, or the question of where it is that the change occurs. These are difficult questions. A change is always relative to something which does not change. It is always inside of a sort of dialectics between change and something else. So it is between change and immobility, between change and a different or another change. All of these are possible questions, and they are in fact difficult questions.

I shall begin by a more personal question. Maybe it is the question of my proper change or my proper inability. Here, in the mountains, my attempt will be to transmit something to you, and to discuss something with you. I think that this transmission is first of all a paradoxical one in some sense. And this transmission is also something which is in a relationship with the question of change. And so I will begin within our situation here. What is the sort of situation where my attempt is to transmit and to discuss something with an audience composed of all of you? My goal is probably to change something in you. Or is my goal to transmit something which is already here – which is somewhere, but nonetheless here – and to therefore only give you something that will not really change what you are but will merely attempt to complete what you are?

This transmission is really a question of teaching. Everybody knows that sometimes we are in a difficult and paradoxical situation when we examine the question of teaching. But what I want to examine today are two points concerning the paradoxical situation of teaching, where teaching involves transmitting something to somebody else. These two questions are on the side of the transmitter, myself, and on the side of the audience, you. On the side of the transmitter, the teacher, or the master, there are many names for this position. The transmitter, the teacher, the master, the professor, and so on. First, the transmitter here is an old man. Do not say that I am really a young man [laughter] because it is not true. I know that I am seventy-five years old. And seventy-five years old is really just before eighty. And certainly eighty is really, in our world, the beginning of the last straight line of life. But there is nothing pathetic about it, I am seventy-five years old. Okay. I am probably an old man, but I am a happy old man. But my question is much more precise. My question is: what is the contents of the transmission of something by an old man?

You know it is a historical question because during history – maybe during a very old time – the function of an old man was to transmit. Maybe it is not exactly true today, maybe it has changed. Today it is much more the kingdom of young men and women, and old men are in the past. They are in the old world. But it was different for thousands of years. An old man and an old woman were in a position to transmit something to a young man and a young woman. And so for a long time there was a strong relationship between transmission and age. Generally speaking, there was something sacred in the old man precisely because he was in the position to transmit. What must an old man transmit? Something of his proper experience, the natural contents of a long life. A long life is also a long experience, and the old man can transmit the contents of the long experience to the young men and women who do not have this long experience. But this experience is precisely something of the past. So we know that it is a question of change.

We have here an example of the relationship between the past and the present, the old man and the young man or woman, in an experience of transmission. And it is really a transmission of the experience of the past. Immediately, we have the question of the relationship between the past and the present which is an example of change. So we have the first paradoxical situation: the old man must transmit something which is a past of his or her experience. But this experience is an experience of the past. How can the experience of the past be interesting for the young man or woman of the present? It can not be a pure repetition because if it is there is no necessity to transmit the experience. Classically, the name for that sort of transmission is tradition. It is the traditional experience. We can say that the definition of an old man was his capacity to transmit tradition.

You know the word tradition is near the word transmission. It is also near the word translation, and so on. It is all of that which comes across time, precisely. It comes from the past to the present. But it is much more complex because in tradition there is an idea of a transmission from the past to the present, but finally for the future. Transmission of the past to the present is the idea that the future will be the same thing as the past. It will be a repetition of the past. Tradition is something that does not organize change but rather organizes a sort of struggle against the change. It is the form of something which comes from the past and which is transmitted in the present. The goal is to make certain that the future will not be obscure, unclear, difficult, and uncertain, but instead the same thing as the past. And so tradition is the name for a transmission which is a necessity for the struggle against a change.

It is not an obscure, reactionary, or irrational vision. After all – we will discuss this point – we know that it is possible to have very irrational changes. Change is not a value by itself. For example, if you are in a small human group, and the continuation of life is by itself a problem for you because you have enemies of all sorts, and so on, it is normal in this situation for you not to want change. If you exist at all, it is good. And so we must transmit the conditions of this existence for the future, for the continuation of existence as such. We know that in the small human groups of the past or in the present, tradition is something that goes in the direction of the continuity of the existence of the group. Change is very often something negative because it's something which transforms the conditions of the existence of the group.

So the transmission from an old man to the rest of the group, as a sort of example, is a transmission of something like a struggle. It's not at all pure passivity. Absolutely not. The tradition must be accepted. It is the active vision of the tradition itself. But it is also a struggle against the change. It is really what we can name a conservative change. It is a change toward continuity, conservation. Finally, it is a struggle for repetition. The idea is that change can be, and very often is, something which is not appropriate for the continuation of the existence of the group. And so we have to go from the past toward the present and for a future which will be a sort of repetition of the past. But I insist on the point that this repetition of the past can not be a passive one. We must work and affirm the necessity of the repetition. Many things can change toward a bad direction for the level of collective existence in the case of a small group.

Generally speaking, that sort of transmission, that sort of position of the old man, is meant to organize the youth inside a sort of struggle against the change. It is the struggle to continue the pure existence of the collective. In that sort of vision we are by necessity in the function of the old man or woman of the group. He or she must transmit and organize this struggle, the name of which is tradition. It is a struggle against the change. If he or she does not transmit or organize, something bad may happen to the group itself. All of that is to say that the conflict between tradition and change, between a conservative position and the will to change, is a very complex question. It is not at all a question of struggle against passivity. There is, in the real tradition, something which is also a struggle. We can have a struggle for repetition and not only a struggle for change. The norm is not that one is progressive and the other is conservative, and so on. That is much too simple.

In the tradition we can find the figure of the old man as a master of wisdom. The master of tradition is also a master of wisdom. In fact the master of wisdom is generally a master of immobility, a master of quietness. The master comes from the beginning of humanity, from a very profound past, an eternal past in some sense. The master of wisdom speaks from the point of view of this eternal past and also from the point of view of an eternal repetition. And the old man is always the figure of this mastery. You can not find a very young girl as a master of wisdom in the tradition. Maybe in the future you can find something like that, but not in the past. The classical picture of the master of wisdom is the old man, the man of tradition, the man who can transmit something not only of his proper life but also of the profound past.

In fact, the goal of the master is to change the audience. The goal of the master is not to repeat. In general, the goal of the master of wisdom is to change the subject, to change the young man or the young woman in the direction of repetition. It is also to change the subject in the direction of a sort of conformity to the fundamental stability of the real world. The fundamental stability of nature. The classical position of the old man as a master of wisdom is not to insist on pure repetition, it is to change the mind of the audience in the direction of repetition. It's not the same thing. It is to organize inside the subject the struggle against false change or bad change. And it is to organize in the subject the return to the good repetition, or the good life inside the repetition of nature. For that sort of wisdom the repetition of nature is the real world.

We have here not only the question of the group – I have said that, generally speaking, an old man is in charge of the continuity of the group by the repetition of norms and the struggle against change – but we have also a new problem which is the relationship between the question of change and the question of nature. The modern form of this is the question of ecology. Certainly, in the old tradition, the master of wisdom had the idea that we must be adequate to the movement of nature, adequate to that which is of much more fundamental importance than ourselves. And so we must struggle against subjective change because it is not adequate to the big world of nature. We can find something like that in the classical history of Stoic philosophy. Stoic philosophy is also something like a struggle against the false changes of the subject. We must have a quiet disposition inside the big world of nature.

I can say a few words concerning contemporary ecology. After all, it is the modern form of the discussion concerning the relationship between mankind and nature. The ecological vision today is very often that mankind is moved by a sort of monstrous desire for newness, a monstrous desire for change, which is a desire to change nature itself. And so mankind is destroying nature in some sense, and mankind accepts the risk of the destruction of nature. What exactly is the struggle against that? The profound ecology, which organizes thinking, is a vision of the struggle against the destruction of nature by the infinite potency and desire of mankind. In some sense this vision is a return to a sort of tradition insofar as it is a struggle against change. It is a sort of tradition which claims that we must respect and take care of the universality of nature. We must respect and take care of the natural forms. Living beings are not always human, and we must accept the fact that there is something in nature that has the right to repeat and continue its proper existence. We must allow living beings to escape the destruction of the violent desires of humanity.

In ecology we can find a new form of the question of change. Maybe it is the idea that we must create something like a modern tradition. You must understand the point clearly: the modern tradition is a tradition by the fact that we preserve the repetition of nature in some sense. The repetition is only the immanent continuity of nature, the diversity of nature. We must stop destroying this continuity. We must stop creating monsters, killing without limits, having atomic disasters, and so on. If we must stop destroying nature we must accept the law of continuation in some sense. This is why I speak of a modern tradition.

If we want we can compare this to the classical revolutionary vision because the classical revolutionary vision is absolutely on the side of change. In some sense, the revolutionary vision accepts the idea that we must destroy the old world. But to destroy the old world is also to destroy the old nature and to submit nature completely to the new revolutionary change. It is not only an abstract vision, it is a real desire. The revolutionary desire has no proper respect for the universality of nature as such. First of all, there is no respect concerning human lives. In the classical revolutionary tradition the position is not only that we can kill, it is that we must kill. Kill, because the point is to destroy the old world and to create something new. It is to create something new inside and by the movement of the destruction of the old world. In all of this nature is passivity, repetition, and not at all inside the revolutionary change.

This is why ecology is not directly inside the classical revolutionary vision. Ecology is something different because it is a traditional revolution. It is a revolution of the tradition itself. Ecology aims to create a new tradition. It does not aim to create a new form of pure progress or of pure becoming. You know it is a very complex and interesting question, this relationship between the sort of will for a new tradition and the revolutionary tradition. So we can say that ecology is the attempt to create a revolution of the revolutionary tradition, it is the attempt to invent a new tradition. It is also something which is a critique of the revolutionary tradition. What I name the classical revolutionary vision is also in some sense a tradition. It is a tradition of change. But we can see immediately that in ecology we have the desire for a new tradition, inside of which there is the possibility of a future which is not only composed of change but also of continuity and repetition.

It is a very new problem. You understand, there is a metaphysical question inside all of this. It is the question of the relationship between nature and history. The modern world can be defined as a world that does not accept that history is based on repetition. This is the most important definition of what is called modern. The contemporary world is only a part or stage of this modern world. Humanity does not accept that history is based on tradition and that history is repetition. The contemporary world believes that everything based on repetition and tradition must be destroyed. And so history becomes completely different from nature. The contemporary world affirms that the laws of history are not the laws of nature. Inside of this vision, humanity develops the idea that history is a struggle against nature, and that the price of historical change is largely to destroy some parts of nature. It is a question of technological invention, of *techne* for Heidegger, whereby the technique is the devastation and destruction of humanity or being itself and not only of the devastation and destruction of nature.

It is a nihilistic activity. The real question is if our historical world is nihilistic. Certainly, the world is not adequate to the laws of nature as such. Our vision of history is that we can destroy some parts of nature. We can also destroy the traditional past of humanity itself because the struggle against nature is also the struggle against tradition. It is also the struggle against human traditions. For example, we destroyed small groups. We destroyed small groups in a very short time, in a matter of some centuries, and this is practically no time at all. In a few centuries we may have destroyed many languages, small groups, and civilizations, to create what we now know as the modern world. It is a question of change and repetition. It is true that the modern world is not only the revolutionary world but is also the capitalist world. And it is true that the capitalist world is also, first of all, destroying a large part of nature. Today we all accept in some sense that our history can not be a pure repetition and it can not be based on tradition. In three or four centuries of the history of capitalism we have destroyed enormous quantities of living beings, civilizations, small groups, languages, and so on.

Nobody today accepts the return to a world based on pure repetition and pure tradition. Even the will of ecology is not to return to the old world based on pure traditional transmission. So the position of ecology is really to create a new tradition. It is not to repeat old traditions, but to create a new modern tradition. This is why ecology sometimes finds itself on the side of classical wisdom. The problem of this creation of a new tradition is that perhaps it is not a tradition for the old man of past traditions, and perhaps it is a tradition for young men and women of the present tradition. It is a paradoxical tradition but we must accept it. It's a tradition which is not a movement from the past to the present, but is much more like a movement from the present directly to the future. It is an attempt to create a future which is not the continuation of pure change, of destructive change.

The question is: why must we refuse to destroy nature? And the difficult point inside all of this is: what is the historical vision of ecology? We can understand that its natural vision maintains that it is very dangerous and horrible to completely destroy nature. We must accept a part of repetition in some sense from the natural tradition because we are human beings inside of nature. The profound idea is that we must refuse the complete separation between history and nature. It is a very difficult point. Ecology proposes a new peace between history and nature which is also the peace between human kind and animals, and so on. It is a new peace inside of all living beings. So the point is that there is a new vision of the relation between history and nature. We can clearly understand the point on the side of nature, it is a claim that we should not destroy nature. But what is the effect of all of that on the other side, on the conception of history? What is the historical vision of ecology? This is the truly difficult problem.

It is a rupture with the modern world because the modern world separates history and nature. For example, the affirmation by Descartes was that human kind is the master of nature. And so nature is not the problem. We can destroy, we can take what we want from nature, and so on. With ecology we have the affirmation of another conception, and this conception is a rupture with the modern world. It is the affirmation of a new peace with nature. But what is the historical vision of ecology? After all, it is a philosophical problem. Is it possible today to invent or to create a completely new historical vision which includes a sort of peace with nature? In the peace treaty with nature, mankind is on two sides. And this is the problem. Nature is mute, nature does not say anything, nature does not speak at all. So, it is a negotiation of human kind with itself.

It is a historical vision in which we discuss and examine the relationship between history and nature. But it is very important to observe that we can not think a new relationship between history and nature on the side of only nature. It is by necessity on the side of history too. We must presume all of this. It is the ecological problem today, it is the problem of a rupture with the modern world which is also a rupture with the revolutionary tradition. The problem is how to discuss a new relationship with nature inside the historical world and within the modern world. The modern world is the affirmation of the separation of history and nature. It is a very concrete problem. For example, if you decide to protect some animals, how do you do it? How do you protect the animals? To protect the animals you must make purely human decisions. For example, you could put the animals in a quiet place. But you must define the quiet place. Animals will not help you, they do not say anything. You must organize the quietness of the place. Generally, it is a fight. In fact, it is also a war to protect the animals. We must protect animals by purely human means, and maybe often by violent human means.

It is a completely paradoxical situation. All the means of the modern world are mobilized inside the modern world to create a new relationship to nature. Moreover, the means of the modern world are mobilized inside the contradiction of history and nature. This contradiction can not be displaced immediately, it is impossible. That is the first problem. The second problem is the question of destruction. The first problem was the relationship between history and nature, but now we have a second, metaphysical, problem which is the question of nature. What is nature? Ecology is by necessity a new proposition concerning the very notion of nature. It is a change in the definition of nature. This is the most important point, because it is a sort of ontological problem. When we say that we must stop destroying nature, what is the real signification of nature? We can not think of nature as only continuation, repetition, and creation. Nature itself is also death and destruction. Thinking of life is also thinking of death. Certainly, we have destruction and death on the side of history. We also have destruction and death on the side of nature. Nature is the most important serial killer, it is without comparison. Finally, the history of death is practically nothing in comparison of death in nature. Nature is the most important potency of death.

When we propose a peace treaty with nature it is in some sense a negotiation between two killers. And so ecology must be a meditation of death. Very often ecology prefers to be a meditation of life. But we can not escape the philosophical problem of the dialectical relationship between life and death at the nature level of our being. Nature is able to destroy mankind and the complete world of living beings. You know those fascinating dinosaurs. It was a world for them, a complete world. The world of reptiles is a complete and fascinating world. We love dinosaurs, but because they are dead, because nature did the job and killed all of them. It was the complete destruction of a complete world of living existence on our planet.

We are small killers after all. Nature is purely indifferent to the question of life and death. For nature there is dialectical equality between life and death. All life is also the movement of its proper death, and death is also the condition of life. Killers are everywhere in nature, and human kind is certainly also a killer. I think the problem is that it is impossible to find a new tradition where we accept that we are a part of nature and that we have a responsibility concerning nature. It is impossible to do that with a norm which is purely natural, or with a principle or orientation which is only on the side of nature. Nature can not decide by itself between life and death. For nature life and death are at the same level. So if we want to stop destroying nature for reasons which are not completely natural there must be something artificial in ecology itself. It is also a human creation. I think that the destiny of ecology, profound ecology, philosophical ecology, and political ecology, is to propose a new historical vision of nature. It must be a new historical vision of nature which will also be a new meditation on death. What is the exact place of death inside of our vision of humanity, and inside of our vision of nature? That is the new question of wisdom. I accept it as a new question of philosophy.

For a very long time the question of death has been a religious question. We must accept that for millions of people and for many of centuries the question of death has been a religious question. It is a fact. I think that what is obscure in ecology, but what is also promising in it, is the invention of a non-religious question of death. This non-religious question of death will have to be a new measure of the question of destruction. It will have to be something that can give a new measure of the question of destruction, of the question about killing, in relation to nature and history. I think that in our modern world – the world of constant change, constant new inventions, constant destruction – we have no idea about death. We have some fragments of religious visions, we continue to have the religious vision of death. But the religious vision of death is a part of an old tradition, it is only a survival of an old tradition. We have no new vision of death. This is why we can kill. We are without an idea of death. We can kill millions of animals to eat and we can kill millions of people. You understand, we can not find the reason for all of this inside nature for the simple reason that nature too kills without any question.

Maybe the function of the old man and woman of the future will be to transmit a new tradition concerning a possible peace between mankind and nature. Maybe it will concern the new historical vision of death. In our world, death is without any signification. It is a return to pure nonsense. Death is returned to its natural existence. We must die, it is a natural law. It is not a historical law that we must die, it is a natural law. If you want to have a new tradition which is not the repetition of religious traditions then we must find a new sense for death, a new sense for the relationship between life and death. The very complex proposition of ecology works in this direction. What is the relationship between life and death from a historical point of view and not only as a natural law? This is the way of giving nature another sense, one inside a new historical determination.

The initial question was about the possibility of an old man or woman as the transmitter of the future. It concerned the possibility of what I can name a philosophical tradition, and it concerned the philosophical transmission of the question of what it is to live with death. It also concerned the possibility of participating in the transmission of a new idea, a new historical idea, an idea concerning the relationship of human history to nature. That is an open question. It is your question and not the question of the old man. It is the question of the future. We must die, we must die. It is inside of human history and it is something which is of purely natural origin, and so if we want to modify the relationship between history and nature we must modify our relationship also to death. It was the religious vision of the old tradition, absolutely. Maybe we can continue the religious tradition, but you know that there is a contradiction between the modern world and that sort of continuation. It is an old tradition.

The new tradition, which does not exist, is a new treaty between history and nature. It is the possibility of a new tradition. The first part of the history of mankind has included the idea that mankind is inside nature. It's a case of small groups, but small groups are the major part of the existence of mankind. Pure history is something very short. Maybe it is a pure transition. It was the idea that we are inside nature, and so humanity is a sort of negotiation with nature, a sort of closed immanent relationship. For example, it is why, when we see the magnificent pictures of animals on the walls of caves from pre-historical nature, we can say that the world of animals is constitutive, that the world of animals is the world in fact. After that we have the progressive construction of radical difference between history and nature. It is the slow operation of the modern world.

We can say that one form of all that is the big states, the empires, and so on. This is the affirmation of power, of history as collective power, of power from all people, and also the power of nature. It is the second part of the existence of humanity. The first part is pre-historical, the second is historical. And the third is our creation, it is our possibility. Maybe if we don't invent a new treaty with nature, a new treaty concerning the relationship between life and death, maybe we will die like the dinosaurs. It's a possibility. Maybe from the point of view of *after,* mankind is not so marvellous. Maybe dinosaurs will come after mankind again. And so I think we must find something new. We can not continue for very much longer to destroy and kill as we do. But we do not have the means to do anything else today. We do not have the means to do anything else today because we do not have a clear idea about a new relationship to life and death. This is really the fundamental problem. So your task, our task, is to open up the third stage of the existence of mankind. It is not a small task. It is why we are always in search of something today, why we live with uncertainty, it is why we are on such an obscure world.

It is absolutely the question of change. And it will be one of our more important questions. You know, you have here two different visions about what constitutes change. In some sense, in the modern world, there is always a new change. There is the world of change. New products, new inventions, new technologies, new populations, and so on. It is a world of new change, a world of constant change. When I say that we must find something new – the change – it is not the same change. It is not the change that is inside the change of the modern world but a change of the modern world itself. And so we come to the conclusion that change has two different meanings. First, the change inside the world as it is, the change inside the modern world, the change as a law of the world as it is, which is, finally, the great law of the modern world: change or perish. That sort of change is something like a law, it is change as the law of the world.

It is completely different from the change of the world itself. The second change is not a change as the law of the world, it is the change of the law of change, and so the change of the world. We must change a world, the law of which is change. Today we are inside of a crisis of change. But the crisis is only a lesson concerning change as a law of our world. All of our governments are working for the return of change, the return of normal change, and against catastrophic change. They want the return to the law of change. In fact, it is also the catastrophic law because the next catastrophe will be for the others. We must understand what a crisis is while understanding that the law of our world is constant change, constant progress, invention, circulation of money, and so on. It is a very constant and weak form of change.

If we want to change radically with the world we must by necessity create a world which is not exactly under the law of change. In some sense, a world which is under the law of change is the same world. We must introduce a tradition, not as a law of the world, but as something which is a limit to the absoluteness of change. We must create a dialectical world, we must create a world which is the reality of a dialectics between change and tradition. That is the point. To create a world that is something like the dialectical relationship between change and tradition – a world where there is a clear and universal measure concerning the question of destruction, killing, and so on – we must have a new idea concerning the meaning of life and death.

So it must be a new idea concerning nature. It must concern the natural part of human kind. That is the condition required in order to have a new idea of the relationship between history and nature. This is the ecological problem. It is why I can describe the future old man from the present. If the future of all of that is the transmitter of the tradition of the new world, it is also a transmission of a new relationship between tradition and change, and, finally, a new relationship between life and death. The transmission of a new relationship between life and death comes from the position of something like a philosophical tradition or a dialectical tradition. A dialectical tradition is a tradition in which we accept the relationship between tradition and change. A dialectical tradition is not repetition, it is the preservation of the new relationship between tradition and change. It fixes the limit point at the barbarism of pure change.

There is no real civilization in the modern world. The modern world is savage. It is why today there is no tradition properly speaking. There is only the continuity of old traditions. There is no tradition because pure change is without any tradition and without any civilization. Tradition was also civilization. It came with something static, something oppressive, something conservative. Today there is only the struggle for change and the struggle for life. A new civilization is a new treaty between history and nature, it is a new treaty between tradition and change. And if the new treaty does not come from the religious dimension you can say that it is something simply philosophical.

I hope that you will some day create a philosophical tradition. I am only a transmitter of the future, of the possibility for you, and for your daughters and sons, to create a philosophical tradition. For the moment philosophy exists, but there is no philosophical tradition in the sense that I propose here for you. Certainly, there is a religious tradition, there is a scientific tradition, but something like a philosophical tradition – which is another name for a dialectical tradition – does not exist. And so, finally, I am the prophet of the possibility for a new philosophical tradition. We stop here.

Seminar Two

*Everybody hates Plato, except for me * Identity & difference * The generic audience*
*Universal change * There is no price for a truth * Prisoners of difference*
*Desire for the Monster * Moving across differences*

We will begin with the issues concerning the organization of our collective world. Immediately, there are many questions. And there is the possibility for a discussion. So we must organize all of that. I propose to have two days of collective discussions. So the situation is very simple. If you have a question, you will write it down and give it to me, and after that we will discuss the question in two special sessions. You can give me the question whenever you want, whenever you see me. I have two further points: first, you should write the question clearly so that I can read it; second, you should put your name. Naturally, the question can be anonymous. It can be a question from the profound past, from nature, for example. It can be a mystery. Generally, the question is from somebody, so give your name. After that we will organize our discussion. So we will have two moments of discussion. For the first moment you can give me the question today or tomorrow. After that, we have other possibilities.

I return to our main problem, change. Abstractly, we shall have three great questions. First, what exactly is a change? I would like to find a clear definition of what constitutes change in the classical philosophical method. Inside this question, we have the question of different forms of change. For example, there is change as a law of the world and there is change as a change of the laws of the world. These are two forms of change. Are they exactly the same? Are they different? Why are they different? These are the first set of questions. We also return to the question of tradition and to the question of repetition, because the question of change is very often the question of the relationship between change and repetition. This is the first group of questions.

The second group of questions will concern the orientation of change. What is the orientation of change? What is the possibility to think the change at the level of a global orientation of different forms of changes? We also have the question of the rationality of change, the question of the thinking of change? What is the space of thinking in relation to a real change? It is a true question because there is a philosophical tradition which claims that it is in some sense impossible to think change as such. But when we think something it is always because we think the part of the change which is not changing, properly speaking. For example, it is the position of Plato. Plato thinks that change as such can not be solved. The question of thinking is precisely to find the part of the existing totality which is outside of the change in some sense. The first remark on this point is that our world is the world of change. It is very difficult for us to interpret the thinking of a pure absence of change because we are completely inside the world of change. For us, change is absolutely natural. It is why Plato has been the enemy of all forms of philosophy for the last century. It has been the case of Nietzsche and the Marxists against Plato. Everybody hates Plato, except for me.

If you say that something changes you have to prove that it is not the substitution of something with something else, you have to prove that something really does change. We can not argue that something changes without having any identification of the thing which has changed. If the thing changed, it is in some sense the same thing which changed. If this is not the case we only have successive beings which are different. In this case we can claim that we have not properly changed something, we have different things. When we affirm that we are thinking about something which changed we also have to give a proof that there really is something and not only the change. It is a question about the the most classical problem of dialectical thinking, which is the relationship between identity and difference. We can affirm that all problems are probably reducible in form to the problem of the relationship between identity and difference. If we are thinking about the orientations of change we are also thinking about the relationship between identity and difference inside of the change. If change is pure difference without any identity then it is not change, it is difference. In this case it consists of successive differences without identity.

It is a classical problem relating to the personality of somebody. In some sense I am the same as myself. This is a very old and very complicated question. Today it is the question of genetic combinations. In the question of the orientation of change, do we really think of change as such inside the global movement of transformation? The sub-question is: do we have a norm or principle to have an evaluation or judgment concerning an orientation of change? Can we propose to distinguish between positive change and negative change? Finally, this is the most important question. On this point there are different positions. For example, we can have the position that change is bad. This is largely the classical or traditional position. We must be suspicious of every change. We also have the position that change is good. The idea that change is good is even a part of the revolutionary position, because the absence of change is death. After that, we can have the position that some changes are good and some changes are bad. It is a question of context in the global orientation.

Our attempt will be to unify the three questions and to locate the root of the problem. What exactly is a change? Do we have a definition of change? What is an orientation of change? What is the condition for thinking change? How do you get some norms to judge the change? Answering these questions will be the consequence of my existence here as an old man. You know that a small question can in fact become a large question. My second question is a very particular one. It is also a paradoxical question. It is the question of the audience, and so the question of your existence rather than my existence. The question is, why are you here? I am here to teach, to transmit something, but you are also here. And so that is the question. For many reasons, it is a paradoxical question. By the definition of the European Graduate School, a class is not exactly a class in the common sense definition. A class is what I name a generic set. Why a generic set? It is because a generic set, superficially, is a set with elements which are not defined by any precise property. This is a largely negative definition of a generic set. It is a set of elements, and this set of elements is not defined by a precise property.

You know that it is not the principle of identity which defines a set. It is not because you are all the same that you are here. It is specifically true for the European Graduate School because you are not defined here by your nationality, generation, sex, and so on. And so it is difficult to give this class a definition with a property. You are here because you are here. You have many different motivations and trajectories. There is no constant, no property, which defines your presence here. And so, you are a generic set. If you are a generic set, how is it that I can suppose that the question of change is the same question for all of you? Maybe the context of your existence is completely different for all of you. And so the change is also always relative to a context or situation. Maybe the question of change has a different answer for each one of you. This is because change is always relative to what I name the world. For example, the world can be the complete world where you exist, one by one. If you are a generic set then there is no common property of your different worlds, there is no common property which constitutes all of you as a unified set. Maybe the question of change is too abstract to be transmitted to you because you must translate the question through the situation, world, nationality, sex, difference of age, and so on. Concretely, the question of change is completely different.

We are left to construct the question completely at the abstract level. From the point of view of the audience, the paradoxical question is about the transmission of something to a generic audience. In fact, inside of tradition it is impossible to do this. Inside of tradition you must transmit the tradition to a group which is historically inside the possibility of this tradition. There is a close relationship between tradition – which is the question of change in its negative vision – and the question of the determination of the collective or the common property of the collective. In the traditional vision there is always also a hypothesis concerning the group. We know perfectly well that a tradition consists of the same conviction as a national tradition, or that the tradition is a tradition for my small group and not for the other small group. Here, we have the argument of the relationship between identity and the question of change or the question of tradition.

If you are a generic set of human beings, or a generic set of humanity, you are not the audience for something traditional in this orientation. You know, it has been the great historical question: is it possible to transmit something to a generic audience, to an audience which is not defined by a common property or by a specific and particular property? The first person to propose something completely new on this point was the prophet, Paul [the apostle]. Paul, for the first time, claimed that the new religion, the new religious context, and the new religious proposition – not the Christian one, because Christianity was something after – was strictly for a generic audience. It was not for the Romans, Jews, slaves or masters, or for women or man. It was for everybody. And everybody is something which was not really defined. Somebody was always with specific and particular properties. Somebody, for Paul, was a Roman, Jew, slave or master, or a woman or man, or different compositions of all of those. Somebody is defined by particular properties. Paul affirmed that somebody is always defined, but what Paul said was for everybody. It was for something which is not defined.

The radical newness of the religious invention of Paul concerned the religious proposition without any constitutive audience, without any particular designation. It was for everybody. It was for a generic set. Many people do not understand this point, and this is why there has been a long-time refusal of his position. For them, there exists Romans, Jews, and so on. There exists only particularities and the generic set of humanity does not exist. It does not exist because we can not give a name to it. When we say that a person is of the Roman empire, we have a very clear idea of what that means. But when we say that this person is a part of a generic set, we can not not identify the destination of the message. And so the question of change is very difficult to evaluate when what we have in front of us is a generic set, and when it is a question of a change which is universal in nature.

A universal change is a change with some interest for a generic set. There is an intellectual war between the affirmation that every change is for a specific part of humanity – it is the national, ideological, and cultural vision – and the affirmation that there exists changes that are for generic sets, generic humanity, and so for everybody. After Saint Paul, the other example is perhaps Marx. Marx is the modern example. Marx introduced a completely new affirmation that politics must be universal, politics must be international. Internationalism is a name for the generic. In fact, Marx used the word generic when he described the proletariat as the generic class. It was the class which is the foundation of humanity as such.

In the two cases of revolution – the religious revolution in one case and in another case the political revolution – there is an acceptance of the idea of change addressed to a generic set. It is the question of universal change addressed to the generic set and it is also the question of the relationship between change and the world. What is the world, inside of which we have change? The first orientation is to say that change is always a change of a precise world. That is . . .

[A whiteboard crashes to the ground behind Badiou]

Student: First, we abolish the law of gravity.

Badiou: This illustrates the question of change in a very concrete manner. Also, you remember the question of nature? No man or woman was inside this destruction. It was a purely natural phenomenon. We said that nature is also a killer.

I return to the point. The question of revolution, which is also in some sense a generic revolution, a revolution for a generic audience, is a new idea because it affirms that the change is a change inside a specific world. We can define the change because it is a change in the world, it is a change for a set which is not generic but is precisely defined. We can have something like a national revolution, we can have something like a new religious framework which is destined for a specific part of humanity such as the western world or the eastern world. But we can not have a change that is truly universal. The most important attempts to create a universal message of change or a universal revolution are really quite exceptional. There may have only been three or four in the history of humanity.

We can say that the question of universal change is a change which is something good for humanity as such without any specific determination. The question of universal change is in a sense a question of profound transformation. If our question is really to find a rupture or to organize a rupture with the modern world insofar as we define a new dialectical relationship between tradition and change, then that sort of affirmation is probably universal in nature. It is very difficult to say that something like that is only for a specific world or a specific part of humanity. Certainly, it is something which considers humanity as a generic set precisely from the point of view of the message or proposition.

The paradoxical existence of the audience is important for me because the question of the generic set is very important. The question of the generic set is very important because for me it is a truth. A truth is always a generic set. You can understand this point differently, but at the first level it is very simple: if truth is not a generic set, a truth is only particular, a truth is only appropriate to a specific part of humanity, and so a truth is not a truth. It is possible to affirm that there is no truth at all, that there exists only some affirmation, information, or some opinion, and that everything is particular. It is a possibility. This is probably the dominant idea today. In my opinion, it is probably the dominant idea today because capitalism as such has no use for the idea of truth. It is an idea without any profit or promise. It is an idea which is not interesting because it is generic, and so it is not for you or your family. It is for everybody. It is an idea without a price at all and so we can not say that this idea is from the big market. There is no price for a truth.

You can justify the close relationship between the idea of truth and the idea of the generic set. If you think that there exists no truth you also think that there exists no generic set. There are only specific or particular communities but there is no generic set and so there is no truth because truth is in the form of a generic set and for a generic set. The consequence is that if you constitute a generic set you can also speak of a truth. You can object that for you there is no truth. Why is this so important for the general field of philosophy and for the question of change? If something like a truth exists there also exists something which can not change. It is a difficult point. A truth can not change because if it could it would be of only historical nature. If a truth could change it would only be a truth for a sequence of time and not for another sequence of time. If a truth is in the form of a generic set, and if the audience of the truth is everybody, then we must conclude that in some sense a truth is eternal. This is another way to state that the truth can not change. Maybe a truth can disappear for a moment, but it does not change. We can say that the eternal truth in our world is something like a paradoxical reality because our world is a world of change. Our world is not at all a world for truth. It is why the question of a generic set is a question of truth, it is why the question of the generic set is such a very important question today. I insist on this point.

There is very often the confusion that a generic set is a set without differences, that it is something like the claim that everybody is the same. Not at all. On the contrary, a generic set is not at all the uniformity of all elements. It contains all differences. For example, you constitute a generic set not because you are the same but because you are all different. This objection against truth – the objection that truth supposes that everybody is the same as everybody – is absolutely false. On the contrary, truth includes everybody in a place, and that place is of his or her particularity. A truth is not at all the suppression of differences. When Paul claimed that the truth is not for Romans, Jews, women, or men, but for everybody, he was not claiming that the audience of truth is composed of a specific category. He was claiming that the truth goes across all differences. Truth must be accepted by completely different human beings.

The idea of a generic set is also the idea of a complete emancipation of differences. If we have no truth then all differences are enclosed in their difference. And so they are prisoners of difference. A truth is a difference with the freedom of something which is beyond difference. It is not the suppression of difference but the difference with something not reducible to the difference. Inside of the differences we can speak of truth in a common language without any renunciation of the differences as such. It is why I suggest the emancipation of difference.

I return for a moment to the precise definition of the generic set. We must underline this definition in order to completely understand the very important question of the possibility of universal change. The possibility of universal change is also the possibility of politics, artistic creativity, and so on. When you create something you always create something with the idea of the universal audience in mind. You do not say that you are creating something for a small part of humanity which is defined privately.

I suppose the importance of the generic set and of truth. I suppose that the most important human desire of human beings is the desire of truth. Why? It is because true desire is always the desire for something exceptional. For example, in the most common experience of a love encounter the desire at the end is a desire for something exceptional. By exception I mean something not reducible to properties which are clear from the very beginning. It is exceptional in regard to the law. In classical theater, this is why we always have the conflict between the young lovers and the tradition. Many pieces of theater exhibit a conflict between lovers in an exceptional situation who desire change and the tradition which claims that love is not a good thing. Between the potency of the father and love there is a vivid contradiction. But why? It is because the lovers claim that their love is not inside tradition, not the result of the law, but rather exceptional or a pure encounter. And so in some sense the idea of love is generic. They can not construct their lives under the prescription of particularities. They must accept a pure and hazardous encounter with somebody of a generic nature.

You have the same thing in the creation of a work of art. There is also – in the creation of a work of art – the desire to create something exceptional which is not the mechanical result of laws or the illustration of tradition. We can suppose that inside of our world the point is that we desire change, but it is not the change under the law of change. You must understand this point, we create not only products for consumption. We also want something exceptional in regard to the laws of the world or the laws of change. So it is a profound desire for something exceptional, and, finally, it is a profound desire for something which is of generic nature and not prescribed by the particularity of the world itself. If we suppose that a monster is that which does not conform to the law of the world, then true desire is always the desire for a monster.

It is a common experience. When you discuss what has really been important for you in your life, you never claim that it was something normal. You never claim that what has been really important in your life was that one day in particular when your workplace was exactly as it always has been. No, it is always your encounter with somebody, and very often, it is your encounter with tragic events as well. For example, when I had discussions with my two grandfathers during the moment of their lives, they described the exceptional moment of war. For them, it was the war. It is not because they were sympathetic to the war, not at all. It was something terrible. But it was something which was not so terrible that it could be reduced to the common laws of existence. It was exceptional and it was generic in the sense that it was the same thing for all subjects. It was an experience of life which was generic in some sense.

I think that the most profound desire of the human being is the desire for that sort of monster. Even if it is sometimes also a refusal of something which is too terrible. Maybe all true desire is terrible in some sense. And so we can not have the true desire of something exceptional in our life without also having something like fear. We can say that if it is true that the very important desire of the human being is the desire for the monster then we have a contradictory relationship, a dialectical relationship, between desire and love, desire and repetition, and desire and particularity. We desire something beyond normality. This is why the traditional and religious point of view is that desire is not a real thing. It is because desire is always desire for something outside of the law. There is no normal desire, there does not exist a purely normal desire. All desire is a desire for the generic and as such it is not the desire inside the laws of particularities.

Now, I can explain a theory without any technical means. Suppose you have a set ... [Badiou laughs with his audience] … with no technical means! Suppose you have a set, a normal and indifferent set. It is absolutely possible to formalize the idea of a subset of the set which is completely defined by some property. We are completely at the general level. Suppose we search to define the subset of the set. Suppose that this subset of the set is absolutely constructable by means of language. The elements of the subset are all defined by the same property. It is absolutely possible to clearly define that sort of construction. We can clearly define what constitutes the subset of a set which is completely defined by a specific property. It is very simple. We can say that the subset is constructable. It is a name chosen by the great logician [Kurt] Gödel.

Gödel named this kind of subset a constructable set. A constructable set is a constructable subset of the set. When we have the general means to define what a constructable set is, then the question becomes the following: are all sets constructable? It is a possible mathematical axiom to affirm that all sets are constructable. It provides a constructable universe. There is a very interesting demonstration from Gödel that proves that we can not refute the idea that all sets are constructable. We can not refute it. We can give a proof that it is impossible to prove that it is not true that all sets are constructable. The miracle of mathematics is that we can have a demonstration concerning the possibility to affirm that all sets are constructable can not be disproved.

It is possible for mathematicians to claim that all sets are constructable. It is a very clear possibility. It is also a very pleasant possibility if you believe that all sets can be defined by a very explicit property. In this case, this form of mathematics is very clear because there is no room for something undefined, unclear. We are in a very clear universe where we can associate a set to a formula of the language because all sets correspond to a property. We have a direct relationship between an explicit property of elements and a set. The interesting fact is that there are many consequences of this vision for problems in mathematics. Many of these problems are solved if we accept the idea that all sets are constructable. Not only is there a complete relationship between language and ontology but in this situation we can solve many of the difficult problems of classical mathematics.

The really interesting point is that practically no mathematician accepts this vision. This is a very clear and sympathetic vision where most problems are solved. But mathematicians do not accept the idea of the constructable set. Naturally, they study the constructable set – this is an interesting problem to examine – but practically no mathematician claims that the universal set is a constructable universe. And so the desire of the mathematician is to not accept this law. This is a very accurate point. The desire of the mathematician is to not accept the clear constructable universe but to go beyond it and to find the monster. Finally, the monster is the non-constructable set.

After Gödel, and after the idea of the constructable universe, the history of set theory became the history of the search for the monster. That is, it became the search for a universe where it is not true that every set is constructable. It is a complex desire because, precisely, we can not really find a non-constructable set. To find a constructable set is very easy because it is a case of finding the formula or property and taking the constructable universe corresponding to this property. But to find a set that is not defined by a property is the clearest point of the structure of desire. The point is to find something, or to desire something, which is not constructable from the world as it is, but is much rather non-constructable and therefore exceptional.

It is also the law of artistic creation. The point is to construct or create something which was before the construction non-constructable. The progress of the history of art was always to create forms which were not forms before or were not acceptable as forms. And so the entire history of art is a becoming-form of something which was not form. For example, it is the case when we pass from figurative painting to abstract painting. In art and science we have the same history, which is the history of finding something exceptional insofar as it was not constructable through existing means. For mathematicians it was exactly the same story. The question of the constructable universe was completely solved by Gödel. We know exactly what constitutes the constructable universe and that it is a transparent and clear universe.

The desire of mathematicians is not in that sort of universe. Mathematicians go beyond in order to find something else. But what exactly is something else? It was the great mathematic Paul Cohen who solved this problem. By the end of the 1960s, the time before us, the great victory was to find the means to define a generic set. The generic set was the name that Cohen gave to a non-constructable set. It is the miracle of language. When we learn that Marx named the proletariat "generic" a century earlier, and that it was the properly universal class, we also learned that it was non-constructable, in fact. We learned that the proletariat were not politically constructable in the capitalist world. One century later, in the pure field of mathematics, Cohen described the generic set as a set which is not constructable from the property of language. It is the same desire: the desire to think something which is not reducible to the law of the world or the language of the law, and which is really an invention or creation because it is purely universal.

We can say that the invention of Cohen in the mathematical field is a victory of desire against law. The victory is the claim that one can construct a universe in which some non-constructable set exists. And these non-constructable sets are generic sets. So, in the nineteenth century we have had the question of generic humanity framed as an ontological and political question. During the last century we have the complete realization of the generic set, which is not on the side of the law of the constructable or of language, but is much rather on the wide stage of the non-constructable. Naturally, a generic set is in some sense a mathematical monster, we never claim that "this is a generic set" because this would entail claiming the property of something.

You can always claim that you have a proof that in some universe there exists generic sets, but you can not examine one generic set because one generic set is different from another generic set. And this would be a contradiction precisely because we have no property to distinguish the one from the other. In mathematics, a generic set is a set with all properties and all differences. There is one element which is red and another element which is blue, we have an element which is a man and another element which is a woman, another which is a homosexual, and so on. A generic set is a set which composes its multiplicities from differences. A constructable set is a set which composes its multiplicity with sameness or with one property.

We must understand the political implications from all of this. Certainly, a politics of emancipation or a politics for the rupture of our world of particularities, circulations, prices, and so on, is also a rupture of a desire of something generic, of something which is not reducible to categories. It is a desire of the generic set and of humanity as a generic set. This is a desire to move across differences. I insist that the point of differences – this is a point that is so important today – is also the point of universality. It is not contrary to this point because we can accept differences only if something moves across differences. We can emancipate differences only if a generic set exists, and only if we can accept differences inside of a generic set without any common property. There must only be a common recognition of some truth. For example, the common recognition of some truth might be the truth of the generic set itself or the truth of differences.

The political question of differences is always the question of constructing a common world where differences not only exist but where there also exists a common truth of the existence of differences. It is where everybody accepts all that is exceptional in the world of differences. And so this history of the constructable and generic is not at all an abstract history. Naturally, it is a mathematical history. It is when Cohen went beyond the desire of Gödel. It is very interesting to observe that the creator of constructable sets was in fact mad. Gödel was completely mad. In fact, I can understand that. Here is a closed and purely constructable universe. It is terrible, absolutely terrible, because everything has its place. Nothing can be displaced, you are in the place of your property. If you are a woman, you are in the place of a woman. If you are black, you are in the place of a black. The universe fixes the set where the property exists.

Freedom is absolutely under the condition of a generic set. We can not be free in the constructable universe. You have your place. To have a place is not sufficient to be free. To be free is also to recognize another place and to eventually go to other places. The space must be generic for elementary freedom. When you are enclosed in a purely constructable universe, you are enclosed in something like madness. Gödel himself was convinced that the constructable universe was not the true universe. He was inside it but only as a mad man. His proper and desperate desire was to find a generic set. When Cohen found a generic set, Gödel recognized that it was a fundamentally new stage of the development of mathematical thinking. And so all of this is not without a relationship to the subject of change.

In some sense, a generic set is also a set where we can go across differences without dissolving all change. This is probably the great question of differences. It is an absolute necessity that we open the situation of the possible change of places. For all of that, we must be in non-constructability, but without dissolving all differences into the complete indifferences of places. If you want a recognition of difference, you can not have it without any truth. That is the point. Because it is only from the point of view of the common truth that we can effectively recognize differences, otherwise we only have closed differences and not differences in the same universe. Finally, the point is that for a generic set we must recognize the possibility of changing your place as a part of the common truth. Not only do we recognize the place of differences but we also recognize the change of differences. Without truth, we can not do this. Without truth, by necessity we close the system of differences. Certainly, there is a problem of the right of difference, the right to be different, and the right to affirm difference. Okay, but we also have the right to change difference. It is this second life which supposes that the universe is generic and that there is a common truth.

It is why I am a prophet, really. We can not have a dialectical relationship between tradition and change, between history and nature, and so on, if there does not exist a truth at all. The point from which you can accept and think differences and the change of differences under something which is also the preservation of tradition, this is the point of a truth. Naturally, it was also the idea of Paul and Marx. For Paul it was the point of religious truth and for Marx it was the point of a communist truth. In any case we have a truth which is only under the common and universal truth. It is the truth which claims that not only must you accept differences but you must also accept the game of differences. This is the complete game of politics.

Day Two

Seminar Three

*The old man in the world of change * Genericity, truth, differences * A common world*
*Demonstrating equality * Change in world history * Academicism & glorious failures*
*The state as a fixed point * Political repetition, the victory of the state*
*World, event, truth, change * The passion for destruction*

Good morning. It is the second day. The second day brings with it a change in our relation to the first day. We already have an example of change! Maybe it is a pure repetition, we do not know. Yesterday we had two points of departure. The first concerned the question of what an old man is in the context of the modern world. The other point concerned the modern world of change, the world of the youth.

An old man has his life behind him. And so he is not completely a man of this world. He can not begin something because he is at the end of something. The question of the end is always a very difficult one for the old man in this world. This world is a world of change, it can not have an end. It can not finish. It must continue to change or transform. It must continue to introduce novelties. There is a passion for something new, and we know that the end is also the end of newness. The end is a return to pure repetition. It is why the question of the function of an old man is perhaps restricted to whether or not he is a rich old man. If he is a rich old man then he has a function. If he is a poor man he has no proper function precisely because the classical function was to transmit tradition. Today an old man can support the possibility of being the transmitter of a new dialectics between history and nature, and life and death.

The second point concerned the collectivity in front of the old man, the audience. If the collectivity is only a system of closed differences then everybody is inside the proper difference. They are therefore inside their nationality, gender, social position, and so on. If everybody is inside his or her difference we can not really have the community of the collectivity. We can not have something in common. What I name genericity is the way to get outside this problem of the closure of difference. Genericity is the possibility to have some differences and not only difference as such. It is the possibility of a general understanding of differences. In order to accept differences you must understand the difference. If the difference is obscure or pathological then you can not accept the differences. So you have a common world with strong differences and the possibility of an understanding of many differences as such. To have an understanding of differences as such we must have something like an understanding of genericity. We must have understanding of the multiplicity of differences in the same common place.

The philosophical name of this understanding is truth. This passage of truth across differences constitutes the possibility of a common world with strong differences. This point is central, and it is difficult. In this place, here, today, we have the idea that our community is generic. We accept the possibility of strong subjective and objective differences. The fact is that we can not be defined by a simple formula of identity. We can not be defined by a common identity. If we accept this situation then we have the difficulty of answering the question of change. A change can not be absolute change. This is a very important point. A change is always a change

23

somewhere, it is a change in a situation. It is a change in what I name a world. A pure change is a change by itself, it without a situation. It is an impossibility to think a change without a context of this change. It is impossible to think the change as a global and absolute change.

From the scientific point of view, we know that change is relative to some plane of reference. Change is not absolute, movement is absolute. Movement is always relative to some fixed coordinates and so without some fixed coordinates we can not speak of movement as such. For example, with Galileo, and after that with Einstein, we know that the linear uniform movement, is like immobility. It is a question of coordinates. The beginning of modern physics is relativist directly and not only with Einstein. Einstein's work was the second stage of relativity. And so it is also with Galileo, earlier. In the very beginning, Galileo claimed that you can not see movement as such. This was the key difference between Galileo and Aristotle. Aristotle's vision of movement was an ontological vision insofar as we could separate movement and immobility for ontological reasons. With Galileo and the modern physicists it is impossible to do this. We can only speak of movement and of the more general change inside of a fixed and immobile context.

What exists is not change as such but the relationship between the change and a context or universe in which we speak of change. This point is very important because it is possible that we can not have a common change. Maybe there exists a change from one point but from another point this change does not exist. In any case, we must determine some fixed universe in which we speak of the change. For us to speak of a common change we must have a common world. It is only from inside the common world that we can speak of a common change. The point is practically of an objective or scientific nature and it relates to the fact that there can not exist a change for everybody. There can not exist a purely and absolutely common change. The question is, are we in a common world? It is a problem because maybe we are not in a common ideological, religious, world. For example, the life of the rich and the life of the poor are in some sense different worlds. And so to speak of a common change, we must first determine if a common world exists.

It is why, within politics, we must affirm equality. Yet we know that our world is a world of violence and inequality. But to affirm equality is to also affirm that there is always the possibility to be in a common world, across the inequalities themselves. We suppose that the world of rich people is not the same as the world of poor people. It is a very simple supposition, and it is probably true. The consequence is not by necessity that there does not exist a common change. But there is still the possibility that a common change does not exist. For example, poor people can desire a change that rich people do not desire. In fact, rich people negate this desire. And so the change is not common. From the universal point of view we must affirm that the change is a change for everybody in a political field. We can not hold the idea that we must exterminate our enemies. It is a desperation, in some sense.

We must affirm that there is a point where the change, which is a desire of poor people, is also a good change, for rich people. This affirmation is not for the present, it is for the construction of the future new world. Naturally, we must affirm that this new world is the return of a common change. We can not say that it is for only the specific and private interests of poor people. It is for humanity as such. If we do not say something like that we open the possibility for a very radical violence. That is the difficulty. In the last century the idea of radical violence was accepted as a consequence of the idea that there exists no common world between the enemy and ourselves. This is because the change was defined relatively. And so the change for poor people can not be the same change as rich people. If we do not have the same world, we do not have the same change. The idea was that revolution, which is the revolution of the proletariat, is not a change for the rich people, it is a destruction of their world. But Marx affirmed that the revolution is for humanity, or for nobody. Naturally, there are tactical enemies, but in the strategic vision of a new world there is a common change.

The new world is a result of a political truth. In this sense, it goes across differences and therefore goes across the appearance of different worlds. This is the most important signification of equality. Equality signifies that rich and poor people do not exist because there is a concrete social equality between them. Equality is the affirmation that your action is of universal value. And so it is not good to kill your enemy. If we can not kill him, if it is possible to not kill your enemy, it is much better. It is much, much, better. The idea is that the future world is also for him or her

The sequence of struggle and conflict, and maybe also the sequence of life and death, must be solved as a contradiction and not as something that must continue as the regular state of affairs. It is a paradoxical sequence where the common change takes the form of a struggle. Inside of this struggle we must be absolutely concerned with the idea of equality. The position of the enemy must be considered as a false position and not as an ontological position. But you know that the consequence of relativity in the scientific field introduces a sort of problem. If there is no common world, there is no common change. In fact, ontologically, we can believe that there exists different worlds and that the political process goes across different worlds. We must affirm that the empirical existence of different worlds can not be the law of action. Instead, the law of action is that there exists a truth which goes across these differences. It is the principle of radical equality.

In some sense there has always been a common world. It is the possibility of common change. If we are not able to define the level where a common world exists we also can not propose a change which is not a change of violence. We can not accept that sort of violence, that is my position. It is a violence which results from the in-existence of a common world is at the abstract level also the in-existence of the principle of equality. When we do not affirm the existence of the common level from the point of view of the world, the point where the rich have the same interests with the poor, then we accept violence and reject universality. It is not the violence of a truth but only the violence of some particular interests. The particular interests of the poor people is not a good reason for violence. Poor people must demonstrate from within their proper world that they can propose a level of equality. It must be a level of common conviction concerning the change of the world. This is my first important remark.

There is also a difficulty concerning the possibility of a common conviction of change as a historical problem rather than a problem of the simultaneity of different worlds. A big change in some historical context can be a small modification in another context. I will give you a trivial example: the idea of the abolition of slavery. If you were in the ancient Greek world then the idea of the abolition of slavery would have been such an extraordinary change that nobody proposed it. Slavery was practically a natural law. Good philosophers, such as Aristotle, justified slavery as the rational vision of humanity. During the centuries of antiquity there were no clear oppositions to slavery. At best there were some who claimed that slaves must be treated good, and so they proposed a soft slavery. But today the idea of the abolition of slavery is something of the past, we do not even need to affirm it. Naturally, there is, in some sense, slavery here and there, but it is not constituted as such as a real political problem.

Between the two time periods there have been great wars fought concerning the abolition of slavery. In the United States, during the 19th century, there was the first modern war concerning the principle of slavery. There was an enormous amount of deaths. It was the first great modern massacre. The invention of the modern war brought with it terrible destruction. All of that is simply to claim that we can go from the situation where something like slavery is practically inside the world in a natural manner toward a situation where everybody rejects slavery. The change, which is the name I give to the abolition of slavery, has been practically completed in the current historical context. And so we can have the idea that a change is not only relative to the world where the change does not exist but that it can also be relative to the history of the world. The moment you have a change which is of a very strong nature, at another moment it is practically a small modification.

It is a question of the historical nature of change. So when we propose a change, we must have an idea of the history of that sort of position. We must know the history of the proposition of change. It is why, in politics, we must know something about the history of politics and not only the immediate context. When you propose something of a political nature, you must have an idea of the history of that sort of proposition. It is not very often the case. Many propositions, many revolutionary ideas and conservative ideas, are made without any knowledge of the history of the proposition. It is a question of the change as a problem, and of change identified itself as a problem.

A very important part of scientific activity is the examination of the history of the problem. "This problem has been solved," "this problem is still unsolved," "this problem is near another problem," and so on. It is not in the interests of science to examine a problem that was solved many centuries before. In the scientific field, the history of problems are a part of the knowledge. In some sense, it is the same thing with artistic creation. To propose new forms, to inscribe ideas in new forms, is also an artistic problem. It is not only a problem for science. In artistic creation, we can not repeat the solution of the problems of new forms. When we repeat we are in an academic style, and an academic style is defined by the fact that sometimes we solve artistic problems which were solved years or centuries before. To go beyond academic style – modern academicism or contemporary academicism – we must propose a solution to new problems or else we must solve unresolved old problems. For all of that we must propose a new system of forms.

Academicism is false change. It is a change which is not a new solution to the problem. We can say that the artistic consciousness is a consciousness of artistic problems in some sense. And so artistic creation is inscribed into the historical process. A great artist knows the solution to old problems and knows the new solutions. So creation is also a memory. It is clear in the scientific field and it is also clear in the artistic field. In some sense it is unclear in political activity. It is too obscure in the political field. There are many repetitions in political activity, many false novelties, and many attempts that result in failure. To begin to examine the proposition of change we must have the knowledge of its history. This is also true for a revolt, strike, or protest. It is even true for a revolution. We must know the history of successes and failures. We must know why certain political actions do not provide us with a good result, and so on.

We can not have a purely new consciousness without memory. This is the difficulty of a new change in the political field. In the political field there have been too many repetitions, too many glorious repetitions. There have been too many glorious sacrifices and glorious failures. The history of politics has been full of glorious failures. But these are not virtuous. This is one of the reasons we must have a comparison between artistic creation and political processes. What are the real practical conditions of creation in the artistic and political fields? We know perfectly that we must have a memory and a history of artistic creation. We can not act from a completely new consciousness, it is impossible. There is always a context, and there is some novelty, and there are problems which are solved, and so on. The fear of academicism is a good thing. Everybody claims that you are nothing when you do something which is clearly a repetition in the artistic field. But this is not the case in the political field. In the political field you can do something which has been done many times, and it can once again be a glorious and splendid failure. The question is, why? I think that it is because all of collective existence finds itself in a close relationship to power, all of political existence finds itself in a close relationship to the state.

In the political field this is something which is by its very nature conservative. You know that science and art can not be purely conservative. Science can not be purely conservative because to be scientific is to invent something. This is the law of scientific activity. You must find something new, maybe something small, maybe something big, but you must find something new. There is absolutely no science that intends to affirm something which has already been solved. In this case, there is a strict norm of novelty inside the creative process itself. In artistic creation, it is the same thing. In artistic creation we must affirm a personal or collective style and it must be something new. In the political field, the contradiction consists of the fact that we have a part of the problem which is of a conservative nature. This part of the problem is related to the organization of power in the state.

The state must continue. The question of destroying the state is a question which has enormous consequences. In a changing world we have a fixed point – what I name a fixed point – which is the continuation of the general form of power. If it is necessary, this form of power will continue through violent means, because the state is not only a fixed point but it is a fixed point that can exercise legal violence. Political change is in a dialectical relationship to this fixed point. And so there is always something like a repetition in the political field which can not exist in scientific creation and, in some sense, can also not exist in artistic creation.

In political creation we are always in front of a fixed point. This is the question of power. The question of power is also the question of the continuation of the collective organization as such. The collective organization – maybe it is a good collective organization, or maybe it is a bad collective organization – is a form of power, the law of which is to continue by any means. The law is also the possible violence of the law. Without violence, the law is nothing at all. The law is violent precisely because the state must continue. The continuation of the state is the law of laws. It is the law behind the law insofar as the state is here for the law. You can not have laws without the state.

The state is where you organize the change of the law. It is understood, you can have a change of laws. To change the law is really the classical definition of politics. But we can not have a change of the law without the violence which serves as the change for everybody. All of this is to suggest that the question of change in the political field is much more complex than the question of change in artistic creations or scientific inventions. It is much more complex because the repetition is always a possibility. The struggle against political power, the confrontation with state power, is very often a repetition because the state itself is a repetition. And so the difference is that the law of the state is to be a repetition. The law is to change when we have a struggle against the state, it is to change the state. It is not normal to repeat, but you repeat because the repetitive nature of the state imposes the repetition. I hope that you understand the point as to why there are so many repetitions in political action, why there are so many failures, so many revolts without any real effect, and so many actions which are glorious by themselves but do not produce a real change of the world. Political repetition is the victory of the state.

In our civilized and democratic world – which is not a world of civil war or big revolutions – the real form of the victory is repetition. Political action is in the form of repetition, and this is not nothing. It is a mobilization, a collective moment, it is political life. But it is political life without change because the state imposes repetition in the form of political action. We must know the theoretical part of political action which includes an understanding that political action is an attempt to be as creative as artistic creation. It is the attempt to have many magnificent political works. Works of arts, works of politics. There are very few works of politics in history. There is the French Revolution, and so on, but really there are very few works. There are many glorious works of art but few glorious works of politics.

When we are in political action we must know two things. First, we must know the history of politics. It is the history of repetition as well as the history of a few novelties or creations. Second, we must know the nature of the state: what is the precise relationship between the state and change? What is the dialectics of repetition and change in the field of the action of state power? The law is clear: the general law of power in the form of repetition and change is on one side, and on the other side is history. The state decides and prescribes what is possible. The state, the true power, defines possibilities. Power can be oppressive, it can be defined by violence, and it can also be the state of the law or the government by law. The state has many forms, but it always prescribes what is possible for collective action.

We can find the same thing in the field of art. An academic also defines what is possible in the field of forms. In classical thought art was the imitation of nature. If you did something that was not the imitation of nature then it was thought to be outside of the possibilities of art. It is possible that academicism is something like a state in the field of art. Generally speaking, the academy has no police or armies. Sometimes they can oppress young artists, but their power really consists of prescriptions of what is possible. When you do something that is not possible you must be repressed, absolutely. If we accept the possibilities for collective action as they are defined by the state, then the result is a repetition.

It is not only the question of legality, it is much more profound. It is a question of subjectivity. Is political subjectivity inside the construction of possibility by the state or not? If you accept yourself to be inside of the possibilities defined by the state then you are also inside the repetition of the law itself. There is only one real creative possibility in the political field, it is to do something impossible in the sense of the state. But the sense of the state is the general and collective sense, it is the law of the collective organization. So, it is perfectly clear that in the political field an act of creation must be the affirmation of the possibility of something which is impossible and not only the affirmation of the possibility to do something which is possible. The difference between the two affirmations is sometimes not all that clear. For example, a general strike in our world is something which exists as a possibility for the state. We can have this idea because it is something which does not exist, it is a pure possibility. We can realize the possibility formally but it is too difficult to make it a reality. In some sense, it is the first vision of revolutionary action. That sort of will or political desire is inside state power, it is not a creation. It is the realization of a formal possibility inside power itself.

Naturally, the power insists that the idea of a general strike is not very good. But for the state it is a possibility because there is a right to strike in some form. There must be the realization of the possibility of the creation of a possibility. The creation of a possibility is always the ability to do something which is formally impossible. I have observed that, in the case of scientific or artistic creation, there is very often the possibility to do something which is impossible. For example, the Greek mathematicians created irrational numbers. The very name of it claims that it was impossible. The name is a trace of the impossibility. Or, another example, when the Italian Algebrist created imaginary numbers. The name was also an important trace. All of the very important creations and modifications in the scientific field have been new possibilities, new numbers. For Pythagoreans, it was absolutely impossible to admit the existence of irrational numbers. Irrational numbers were not numbers at all.

You must force the possibility inside of the impossibility. The creation of a new possibility is always to take as possible something impossible. Maybe the true change is always something like that. Maybe it is always something which is not only the first realization of a possibility but also the invention of a new possibility. It is the same for artistic creation. When, for example, you affirm the possibility to take new forms which were before purely in-formal, without form, or were not a pictorial possibility. Or when you create a completely new musical organization like Schoenberg did at the beginning of the last century. In any case, you create forms which were not before recognized as forms, and so you create new possibilities in the field of forms. But to do that you must know the repetitive law of the state. You must understand that the field of possibility is prescribed by the state. We must have the courage to go in the direction of a new possibility.

I would like to examine the problem concerning the difference of points of view concerning change. This is the consequence of general relativity in a non-physical sense. We know we must know history, because the history of change is also the history of the relationship between change and the context of change. We must also know the structure of the state of power, which is the structure of repetition. For a true change, for a change and a new truth, and for a new generic audience, we must know the laws of repetition. I propose to name the context of a change a world. I propose to name the true change in a world an event. An event is always the opening of a new possibility. It is not the realization of a possibility but the creation of a possibility.

And so the question of change occurs between two terms. On one side, the structure of the world – my example was the structure of the state in the political field – is the structure of repetition. On the other side, the event is the creation of a new possibility apparently inside the law of the world. I propose to name the creation that occurs between the two a truth. What happens when there exists an event in a world? There is a process of change which defines the possibility for a new truth. We have three terms to completely understand the question of change. After that, there are many details. But we have a world, which is the place for change. A world is something like a structure. We can describe the general form of a world because it is something like a structure. You have an event, which is a localized rupture in the world. You can think of the event as everything we discussed in terms of creation – artistic, scientific, and political creation. The general form of an event is the creation of a new possibility.

When we have a strong artistic creation, a new general vision of painting or music, it is really the preparation for a new possibility for artistic creation itself. By itself, without this rupture, without this new sense of creativity, we can not have a true change. After that, a truth is a consequence of an event inside the world. This is the most abstract definition that we can understand. A truth is the logic of change and the consequences of change. The recognition of truth is the recognition of the relationship between world and event. The creation, in the world, of a new place for the consequences of the event is the point of truth because an event is a rupture with the laws of the world, so there is no place for the event. There is no place for the new possibility because the state (as the structure of the world) prescribes all of the possibilities. The true change is a change of places and the creation of a new place for a new process. Finally, it is a change of the world itself. If you can create some new places in the world for the development of the consequences of the event, you are really changing the world itself and not only something in the world. It is a change of the question of possibilities for a world, a world which is the structure for possibilities.

In the last century there was the question of revolution, the question of the avant-garde in the artistic field, the question of new forms of science, and so on. In the last century there have been ideas about the possibility to directly create the new world by destroying the old world. It was the great and terrible passion for the last century. It was not only a political passion, it was an artistic passion too insofar as it was a passion to destroy old art. It called for the end of art and for the creation of something absolutely new, a new world of art. It was the belief that artistic creation should be for everybody and that all forms are possible. But it was not the idea to create something new inside the possibility. Not at all. It was the idea that we must destroy the old world and create something new inside its destruction.

Generally, what we saw was the destruction, but the novelty was much more obscure. The novelty was the destruction itself, that was the passion. After that, the contemporary reaction claimed that maybe we must accept the world. We have seen too much destruction, too much death, and too much negativity. We must open up a third moment which occurs after the temptation of the complete negation and total creation of the world. Maybe we must understand the change dialectically. In some sense, it is always inside the world that there is a process. And we can change the world inside the world if we have the consequences of an event.

The question is clear: can we accept the possibility of new possibilities inside the world? It is not the question of the destruction of the world. It is more precise and it involves finding a point where it is possible to go beyond the repetition and to create a new possibility. Always in the world. After that we can have a change of the world within the logic of the consequences of an event. This is why the question of change is so important today. It is not an academic question. The question of change is important because the very conception of change is difficult today. Today, we find ourselves just after the terrible idea of absolute change. The idea of absolute change claimed that one could pass from one world to another world by completely destroying the old world. But there is no old world. The world is neither old nor new, it is a structure which is a repetition and which is the law of repetition. To change the law of repetition we must be inside the repetition by going to the limit of the repetition, to the limit point of the repetition. It is the point where we can propose a new possibility.

And so when we study the change we also study our relationship to the world. This is why the discussion of the world relates to the question of change. We must think on the side of the structure and on the side of creation, simultaneously. The point is not to oppose the two but to understand that there is a possible dialectical vision which does not destroy the possibility of creation with big economies of violence. But I can not promise eternal peace. No, it is not the point.

We will return to this point tomorrow. In fact, we can not create without negation, but we can create with less negation than before, and with less negation than the last century. Less negation, it is my hope. We will begin on this point tomorrow.

Is being qua *being submitted to change? * Parmenides, The false road of negation * Heraclitus, All things are change * Aristotle, The beginning of dialectics * The ontological question & the phenomenological question * Proof by negation, and the negation of negation * Three great orientations concerning change*

After a very long introduction – which was only an attempt to convince you of the importance of the question at hand – we can finally begin to study what a change is. We must know some points regarding the history of the philosophical question of change. We can observe from the very beginning that change – the empirical change of everything that exists, the change of law, the change of the world, the change of the situation, and so on – is probably the most important point of our experience. The meditation concerning change is a constant of all cultures without exception, there is a sort of universal experience of change and a universal meditation concerning the becoming of everything that exists. As a testimony of this, we shall read a great poem from the French poet [Paul] Valéry at the end of the week. It is quite relevant because the poem is explicitly about change, and about the different philosophical possibilities concerning change.

The very nature of change is a fundamental question from the very beginning for philosophy. Maybe it is the first question in some sense. In fact, it is a question which brings with it the first great division of philosophical attitudes. The question of change within the history of philosophy is divided into three great sub-questions. There is an ontological question concerning change. It is the question of being. There is the phenomenological question concerning the empirical evidence of change. Finally, there is the question of the relationship between the two, the relationship between the ontological question of change and the phenomenological question of change. To repeat: there is the question of change at the level of being as such, and the question of change at the level of our experience. And, finally, there is the relationship between the two.

The ontological question has been formulated as the most important question at the beginning of Greek philosophy. The question is: is being as such, being *qua* being, submitted to change? The ontological question concerns the fundamental reality of change at the level of being as such and not at the level of phenomena or the concrete world. Philosophy began with the negative answer from Parmenides. It is very interesting that philosophy began through a pure negation of evidence. It was the heroic decision to affirm that at the end being as such is not submitted to change. Being as such does not change at all. And not only was the position that being as such does not change, it was also a position that being as such is completely unified and so without any multiplicity. This is why the consequence was that being is one. It is the affirmation of the one as such, the pure one. No division, no separation, no movement. The one is the pure affirmation of itself.

I quote Parmenides, "There is one story left, one road: that it is. And on this road there are very many signs that, being, is uncreated and imperishable, whole, unique, unwavering, and complete." This is a very strong and remarkable vision. It is a beginning, really. It is the affirmation of the absolute right of thinking against all empirical evidence. Parmenides knows that our experience proves, on the contrary, that everything changes, and so on. And so there is a sort of imperial affirmation of the right of thinking against all empirical evidence. In some sense the beginning of philosophy is in this affirmation that the truth is not a question of empirical evidence. From this point of view, empirical evidence can be completely false, and we must instead affirm the pure right of thinking within the field of pure thinking.

There is also the idea that if we are in the pure potency of thinking we are also in the pure existence of being as such and not of things, animals, and so on. In fact, there is a sentence from Parmenides which states that thinking and being are the same. From the beginning, then, there is the affirmation that not only is there a right of pure thinking against the empirical evidence, but there is also with this right a way of accessing pure being as such. Finally, we reach the point at which pure thinking and pure being are the same. There is something indistinguishable in the two. When thinking is absolutely the same thing as pure being, we are on the road, the great road, and we observe that have many indications, and finally some proof, that being as such is not submitted to change. This is the profound vision of the one. Finally, the idea is that thinking is always a thinking of the one, the great one.

After that there was a complete philosophical story about the one, because the one became god. The destiny of the philosophical creation of Parmenides was that the one became god. But for Parmenides there was no separation between the one and the world. There is, when we are on the road of thinking, the unification of all that exists including the thinking itself. And so the vision of Parmenides is not itself a theological vision, it is not the vision of a god. It is the vision of being as such, which is not separated from the world. The one is really the form of being when we are on the correct road of thinking and not when we are on the false road. The false road is the road of negation. The idea is that we can only have the conviction that the world changes when we introduce into our experience something which does not exist, the negation. But the negativity does not exist, it is an illusion.

The false road is the road of negation. In fact, the philosophy of Parmenides is the philosophy of pure affirmation. We must begin not by negativity but by an absolute affirmation, and if we begin our thinking by an absolute affirmation then we are in the element of the global one. And so we really have the experience of the complete unity of everything that exists, without any negation. For Parmenides the negation is not real. There is no real negation. We can find something like that from Spinoza, for example. Spinoza explicitly affirmed that there is no negation. We can also find something like that in the contemporary field from Deleuze: negation and reflexive negativity do not exist, they are not a part of the potency of life. Deleuze claimed that non-organic life is without any negation. We find something like that also in Nietzsche. For Nietzsche, true thinking is the great affirmation. All of that has been on the road where our experience is not at all the experience of diversity, multiplicity, and change, but where our fundamental experience is the experience of the one.

First we have the negative answer from Parmenides, and then we have, just after that, the positive answer from Heraclitus. Heraclitus went beyond the choice between being as submitted to change and being as not submitted to change. Heraclitus's position was not a pure opposite to the position of Parmenides. Parmenides claimed that being is not submitted to change, but Heraclitus did not claim that being is submitted to change. Heraclitus claimed that being is change. It is not exactly the same position. Being is by itself pure change. I will quote Heraclitus:

"there is nothing permanent except change." The consequence for Heraclitus was that being is pure multiplicity in some sense. There is no One because if we have something like the One then we have something which is permanent, but there is nothing permanent except change. Something exists only by becoming something else. The very being of something is to become something else. We can not stop the change, and so in some sense nothing exists except for the change of all things.

Heraclitus had the most profound negation of repetition precisely because a repetition is always a repetition of the same and, with Heraclitus, there was no same. We can not understand anything as a repetition of the same because nothing is the same as itself, all things are immediately different from themselves. All things are change. Finally, being itself was only a name for change. You know, by a strange transformation there was a fundamental negation of change in the work of Parmenides. If being is not submitted to change, then we now find that change does not exist. There was no real being of change. And so Parmenides had a pure affirmation, but in some sense the pure affirmation contained a negation. On the other side, Heraclitus had a pure negation because his claim was that there is nothing which exists, there is no One, there is no thing, and so there is only change. For Heraclitus, there was only the constant destruction of everything that exists. But in some sense this is a pure affirmation of change.

The movement of Parmenides was one of pure affirmation as pure negation, and the movement of Heraclitus was one of pure negation as the realization of the pure affirmation of change. You know, we have here the beginning of dialectics insofar as dialectics is the combination of negation and affirmation. We have in Parmenides the immanent transformation of affirmation and negation, and we have in Heraclitus the immanent transformation of negation and affirmation. Finally, the beginning of dialectics is the correlation between the two. The beginning is Parmenides *and* Heraclitus. This is the position of Aristotle. Neither Parmenides nor Heraclitus, but Aristotle.

Aristotle organized an answer to the question through a division: there is a *part* of the world which is not submitted to change. This part of the world which is not submitted to change is god. I quote Aristotle in *Metaphysics:* "there is something which moves without being moved, being eternal substance and actuality." You should recognize the One of Parmenides: something which is eternal, substance, actuality, and which does not move. So there is no movement, there is only unity, pure substantiality, and pure actuality. And so it is something which is not in time. This is the beginning of the philosophical god. After all, the god of creation is the philosophical god, defined as a part of the existent being which is in some sense the Parmenidean part. It is the part without multiplicity, without change, without immanent time, and so on.

There is another part of the world which is of a Heraclitian nature. It is the part which is moved, is not eternal, but is corruptible, submitted to death, and to desperation. It is the part that is submitted to corruption, and which is not pure actuality, but a mixture of actuality and potentiality. The construction of Aristotle's has been a dominant position for many centuries. It was a precise synthesis of Parmenides and Heraclitus's positions concerning change, by an organization of the universe with a part which is not submitted to change and a part which is submitted to change. The relationship between the two positions is the relation of causality.

God is eternal and not moved, but god also moves, and this is the changing part of the world. It is not submitted to change but the change exists by the action of god. It is a strange position: how can something which is not submitted at all to change nonetheless be the cause of all change? There the possibility of something which moves without being moved. We do not have this sort of possibility for Parmenides because the one is not active at all. The one is sufficient by itself, because there is nothing external to it. So, the Parmenidean totality affirms its existence without any external action.

Aristotle's god moves the world, and so it is the causality of change. There are many questions about this construction. Two questions are of interest for us today, because they are questions concerning change. First, is it possible that something which is absolutely immobile can be the cause of a change? This is Aristotle's position. It seems for us that to act is to change because to act is to do something. To act is to do something and to do something is not to remain immobile because doing something involves movement. The change is not by itself a passive change. So when god does something, he is also changing in some sense, and the result of his action is a change. Aristotle claimed that god moves the world because the world is moving in the direction of what is good for it, and so the world is moving in the direction of pure existence. And what is pure existence but god?

Finally, for Aristotle, god does nothing. The world is moved not by the precise action of god but by an attraction *by* god. And so it is really a pure attraction. The world is moved in the direction of its proper good but the goodness of the world is represented by a god which is not in the world. The world is moving because god exists, but not by god. We must interpret Aristotle's claim spatially. God is perfect, and being perfect is a sort of global attraction of the different things in the world because everything in the world is oriented toward its proper good. General good is god, so the world goes in the direction of the perfection, that is, in the direction of god without any action of god.

Aristotle took the contradiction and claimed that it was not a contradiction after all. The contradiction between Parmenides and Heraclitus was not a contradiction for Aristotle, rather, Parmenides knew perfectly one part of the problem and Heraclitus knew perfectly another part of the problem. Aristotle claimed: 'I know all of the problem, and that is why I came after' [laughter] And now I know the problem, it is clear: Parmenides is correct because there is a part of being, the perfect form of being, which is not submitted to change precisely because it is something perfect. And so there is no reason to change. There is another part of the world which is not perfect, which is imperfect, and which is subject to corruption. This part of the world is submitted to change.

To be submitted to change is a proof of imperfection. That was the difference introduced by Aristotle. For Heraclitus change was perfect. But for Aristotle change was not perfect, there was an orientation of the change in the direction of its proper perfection. This proper perfection is represented by god, and so we can say that god moves the world. Aristotle's creation was the conception of a new sort of change – a division in the notion of change – because there was also an orientation of change which claimed that a thing goes in the direction of its perfection, the good. This is the invention of the cause by finality, the cause which is not before the thing but in some sense is the direction of the thing. And it was the great question of change for Aristotle.

Aristotle claimed that there is mechanical change or a transitive cause. We have a cause and we have an effect, this is the field of physical or mechanical causality. But we can not explain the world only with mechanical causality, we must introduce another form of causality which is the causality of god in relation to the world. We call this causality by perfection. This is the idea that everything exists in the direction of its perfection. And it was the optimistic vision of Aristotle. Everything which exists has its proper interest in the good, in the direction of god. Maybe we do not understand our interest, and so we do something which is bad or which is not in the direction of god. But generally speaking we can trust the direction of things toward their perfection.

All of that was the great beginning of the conception of change. First, there was the ontological question, which was answered negatively by Parmenides. This was the pure affirmation of being as such, of being as the one. Second, there was the positive answer from Heraclitus, which was the maturation of the position of negation, the potency of negation. Finally, there was the compromise by Aristotle, who divided the question by the construction of the universe. After all of that, we had the phenomenological question.

I name the phenomenological question the point of departure for the evidence of change. Naturally, in Parmenides we find a complete affirmation of the potency of thinking. But we also have to do something with the evidence of change. As I was saying at the beginning, there is a strong evidence of change which is present in all cultures and in all of the experiences of human beings. This evidence of change is not a question for Heraclitus, and it is not a question for Aristotle. It is not a question for Heraclitus because the evidence is true, everything is change and only change exists. So, for Heraclitus, change is the law of being as such. For Heraclitus, our concrete experience is in fact an ontological experience. There is no difference between ontology and phenomenology with this position. When we have the experience of change, it is in fact our experience of truth, because it is true that being is change. Something of our vital or real experience is also an ontological experience. This was also the conviction of Nietzsche and Deleuze. It is the conviction that our experience of life and our experience of change and becoming is really an ontological truth. It is not something separated from being as such, it is an experience of being. We are inside the great becoming of life.

This position is contrary to the position of Parmenides. Parmenides's position affirmed something which is an absolute contradiction without experience. For Aristotle our experience of change is also a correct experience because we are not god. We are not in the experience of the pure immobility because our experience is the experience of the concrete world of change. It is not a purely ontological experience because it is only an experience of a part of what exists, and so it is not an experience of the totality because it is not an experience of god. Is it possible to have a complete experience within Aristotle's vision? A complete experience is not only an experience of change but also an experience of the existence of god.

Aristotle asked: is it possible to live as an immortal? To live as an immortal is to have an experience of something which is not submitted to change. As you know, the consequence of this vision was the position of mystical knowledge and mystical experience. To be simultaneously Heraclitus and Parmenidean is also to have the mystical experience of god. For Heraclitus, it is when we are in our imperfect world, with corruption, change, and so on, and also, for

Parmenides, it is when we are in the pure intuition of god. These are the contents of mystical experience. The fact that we are within the experience of change is not a problem for Aristotle because our world is submitted to change. For Parmenides, it is a real difficult problem. The difference between the right of thinking and our concrete experience is very large.

Why do we have that experience of change if change does not exist at all? How can we introduce negation into our experience of life? These questions are very important. Parmenides proposed that our experience is purely an illusion, a subjective construction without any ontological value. But what is an illusion and what is the being of an illusion? Parmenides had to demonstrate, if it is possible, that our experience is purely and simply false, that it is non-existent. It was the work of Zeno, the principal disciple of Parmenides, that answered this question. Zeno gave us proof that something like movement, something like multiplicity, does not exist. We will return to this point when we read the poem by [Paul] Valéry. The point is that is it is a proof by negativity that a movement can not exist. If we admit the movement then we are in a contradiction. So a non-direct proof, and a proof which assumes that negation and contradiction can not exist.

You know, this is very important: if you have a proof which is a proof by negation – that is, if you have a non-direct proof – and if you admit that the movement exists, you have admitted a contradiction. The proof is complete only if you affirm that contradiction can not exist. The proof is a proof of contradiction only, and you can have a supplementary principle which is that contradiction does not exist. But in some sense the consequence of claiming that contradiction does not exist is precisely the goal of the proof, because movement is contradiction. Movement and transformation, these are contradictions. The proof of Zeno is a proof and not a condition of the result of the proof.

Why is this proof so fascinating? The result of the proof is to claim that we have contradiction. But the fact that contradiction does not exist is a Parmenidean affirmation. So the proof is only a proof of the fact that the proof is under the condition of the result of the proof. This is spectacular sophistry. And so it is probably not possible to have a proof that contradiction does not exist, because to prove that contradiction does not exist you must have the proof that Parmenides's claim was true, that negation does not exist.

We can not prove that negation does not exist by using negation. It is very complex. The general point is that we must prove that something does not exist. We have many proofs of the existence of god, but, do we have a proof that god does not exist? It is not symmetric, because if you want proof that god does not exist it will not be a positive proof, it will be a proof of a negation. It will be a proof that god does not exist. But if god does not exist at all then how can we have a proof that this entity which does not exist, does not exist? Necessarily, you must turn to the sophistic use of negation.

This is an important point for philosophers because very often we have the temptation to prove that something does not exist. For example, if you are an atheist, then it is good to have a proof that god does not exist. In fact, it is very difficult to find some proof. It is like Zeno's temptation to prove that movement does not exist. The use of negation is always problematic when the proof is a proof that something does not exist. Generally, the proof is circular. You suppose that the thing does not exist to have a proof that the thing does not exist. The question of change is always in a difficult relationship with the question of negation. This was the point of the phenomenological discussion. A change is a negation.

We can not think change without claiming that something is not as it was before. And so we always have a negation inside of the idea of change. It is why Parmenides's idea was to affirm the in-existence of negation. But do you see the complexity? If you affirm the in-existence of negation, you are using negation, in the form of the negation of negation. It is the beginning of the long history of the negation of negation in our discussion of dialectics.

But we should return to the central point which is the relationship between change and negation. I insist on the point that all of the material for the discussion of the concept of change was there at the beginning with Parmenides, Heraclitus, and Aristotle. The true difficulty for Parmenides was the use of negation. If you refute the evidence of experience, with Parmenides, then you have the difficulty of the use of negation. And if you admit negation, you also have to admit change and the possibility that something can be different from itself. If you want to have a historical example of this you can compare the solution to the question of change between Kant and Aristotle. Kant's position was to claim that our experience is not the experience of true being as such. It is the negation of the conclusion reached by Heraclitus. Heraclitus claimed that our experience of change is an ontological one insofar as being as such is change. Kant's point of departure was the reverse: our experience is a subjective experience and there is no reason that our purely subjective experience can be the experience of being as such. So our experience of change – the evidence of change – is subjective evidence.

The problem for Kant was why experience is subjective and yet is also the same for everybody. If the experience is subject then there is no reason why there would be the experience of the same world for everybody. And so there must be a movement – like the day coming after the night – which is for everybody. You know, the difficulty for Kant was the difficulty to think that a purely subjective experience is regular in some sense, or that it is the same for everybody. Kant introduced a structure of subjectivity itself, a human structure which is the same structure of organizing experience. Our experience is subjective but it is also in some sense universal because the structure of experience is the same for everybody, for every subject. There is a sort of structural subjectivity which is the same in every individual, and Kant named this structural subjectivity the transcendental subject. The transcendental subject is that part of our subjectivity which is the same for every subject.

For Kant, our experience of change is subjective and universal. And, maybe being as such is not submitted to change. We can not know. We can not have any pure knowledge of being as such. But Kant admitted that there is a part of being as such that is not submitted to change. He admitted this because he was a religious man. God exists for Kant, and it is an absolute Christian god, it is a god without submission to change. It is a god which creates the world. But we can not know, it is a question of faith. And so we are in Aristotle's vision where there is a part of the world that is submitted to change which is the subjective experience of the world, and there is a part of that which exists which is not submitted to change. And this part which is not submitted to change is god, and we can not really know god. We can not have an experience of god. We must have pure faith. The great question from Kant was the question of the limit of reason. Reason can know only what is presented by experience, but experience is relative to the structure of subjectivity. We have no real knowledge of what is. But by faith, religion, and conviction, and also in the field of imperative morality, we can have another field of experience which is not at all knowledge. It is faith. Faith opens our mind to another world not submitted to change. And, you know, this was Aristotle's vision.

I will conclude for today: from the very beginning we had three great philosophical orientations concerning change. We had the Parmenidean orientation which was also present in some forms of Oriental wisdom with the claim that change is illusion and truth is immobility. Within this position, being as such is not submitted to change. Being as such is a pure continuation of itself and a pure affirmation of itself. Change, multiplicity, and so on, are things which come from our weaknesses. The second great orientation was the affirmation of the universality of change and of being as such as change. The point was to realize the ontological nature of change. Everything that exists exists in the form of a becoming. This is the great orientation of vitalism. Being as such is like a big creature, it is like something which is alive and which has a potency of life. It is the constant change of creation concerning humanity. At the beginning this was the position of Heraclitus, but after that we have many contemporary examples. The third orientation is the recognition of the different levels: a level where change is the law and a level which is not submitted to change.

It is the general framework of the question of change from the very beginning of philosophy. Tomorrow, I will attempt to propose the fourth orientation.

Day Three

Seminar Five

*Why did god create the world? * Being as such is pure multiplicity * Cantor, ontology as mathematics * Physics as the science of change * The ontological principle of extensionality * What is a world? * Objects, identities * "I was not completely myself today" * Existence and being*

I will answer your questions tomorrow. Today I must explain my new solution concerning the question of change.

I already examined the three fundamental positions concerning the question of change. The first position concerning being *qua* being – whereby being as such is not submitted to change – claimed that the empirical evidence of change is a falsity or an illusion. Being is the one and there exists only the one. This was the Parmenidean orientation. The second position was that being is change, whereby the empirical evidence of change is an ontological experience. For this position, the empirical evidence of change is simply a true experience of change. There is no other one than the change itself, but change can not be named the one because it is pure multiplicity. Change is a constant transformation of something into something else. This was the orientation of Heraclitus. The third position claimed that part of being is not submitted to change and part of being is submitted to change. This was the orientation of Aristotle.

The third position was the birth of the properly philosophical and religious concept of god. Aristotle's last book on metaphysics was the first rational and conceptual presentation of the ideal god. After that we have had the complex history of the choice between the philosophical concept of god and the religious concept of god. It is not the same god throughout history. There is the metaphysical concept of god, which is not necessarily a good conception of god for the church because it carries with it something too abstract and rational. You know, after all, the religious question is one of faith and creation. The metaphysical concept of god is something which might be compatible with religion but it is not thereby inside of religion. Beginning with Aristotle, there has been a long and sometimes violent history concerning the relationship between a purely religious conception of god and the rational conception of god.

What is the relationship between an entity which is not submitted to change and the world which is submitted to change and death? For Aristotle there was no creation of the world by god, and so there was no beginning of the world. The world is at it is. If god moves the world then it is evidently by pure attraction. God is the perfection of being, and all imperfect beings are oriented in the direction of perfection. It is not a project of the creation of the world by god. It was, after that, in the tradition of the bible, that there was an idea for the creation of the world. And so the creation of the world was not at all an idea from Greece. In Greek philosophy there was no idea of the creation of the world. At the beginning of philosophy there was only the idea of the possible perfection of a part of being, but not an idea for the creation of the world.

After that there was a complex history of the relationship between philosophy and religion regarding the problem of creation. After all, it really is difficult to understand why god created the world. If god is absolute perfection, and if he is completely perfect by himself, then why did he have this strange idea to create the world? It is an artistic idea, in some sense, because it is perhaps the case that he wanted to create a work of art [laughter]. It is a very interesting problem of thinking about god as a subject. This is not a Greek idea at all, we can not find anything like the idea of god as a subject in the work of Aristotle. God is the perfection of being but he, or it, is not a subject. After Aristotle, we have had the idea of god as a subject, which means that god is not submitted to change. God is immortal, eternal, and so on, but also an active subject. He created the world. The difficulty is to think about a subject which is not at all a final subject but rather an infinite or perfect subject. Why did this perfect subject create the world? The religious response has generally been that the answer is mysterious and without rational explanation.

A French philosopher named [Nicolas] Malebranche proposed a rational understanding of creation as such. I will not provide a lot of detail right now because it is not the point of our topic. But it was the complete absorption of religion by rationality. Malebranche proposed that the creation of the world and also the existence of Christ, the sub-god, could be explained by purely rational means. It was not entirely convincing, but it was really beautiful. It was a beautiful attempt by pure reason to explain not only something very abstract, that is, perfect being, but also the precise determination of a particular religion named Christianity. For Malebranche, Christianity became a rational construction with a sort of transparency whereby nothing was mysterious. We were practically inside of the intellect of god and we could understand the condition of god. We could understand rationally why there was a Parmenidean necessity to create the world and, after that, to save the world by Christ through redemption. All of that was explained by Malebranche. When Malebranche created his explanation he was in front of a rational work of art. I am not convinced of the truth of the Christian religion by Malebranche. However, it was the extraordinary goal of Malebranche to explain that the Christian religion was true not only because of idols, the revelation, the tradition, and so on, but also because it could be explained rationally. This was also the goal of Pascal. It was practically at the same time as Malebranche that Pascal was in the business of determining the truth of the Christian religion by rational means.

All of that was from the third attempt to solve the problem of change by division: part of being is submitted to change and part of being is not submitted to change. We have also seen a variation on this point from Kant. Kant's point was that we can not know being as such and so we can not know if being is submitted to change or not. We can not know any of this because of our human finite thinking. So we must have faith in god. Kant did not have a rational determination of god like Malebranche, but he had faith in god. Our experience of change is the result of an active and universal structure which is a subjective structure of knowledge. So knowledge is in fact the result of a transcendental structure which organizes the appearance of being under some law. But we can not claim that these laws are the laws of being, that is not the point. Laws are laws of our reception of being. We can not really know true being, we can only know that it is possible by the transcendental structure of our knowledge.

And so it is the subject which constitutes the law of change. The conclusion is that change is rational, and we can know the law of change but we can not affirm that our knowledge of the laws of change is absolute. We can not know that our knowledge of the laws of change is the true knowledge of change because it is relative to our possibilities of knowing and relative to the transcendental constitution of the subject. In some sense being as such becomes something obscure and something hidden in the structure of our knowledge.

The fundamental concept of the Parmenidean orientation is the one. The fundamental concept of the Heraclitian orientation is the pure multiplicity. There is no one at all because there is only the constant change of the multiple. We can summarize the orientation of Aristotle and Kant by claiming that the fundamental concepts are the one and the multiple. We can also claim that for Parmenides the point was that of identity. That is, being is fundamentally the same as itself, and so we can not change because being remains within its proper identity. So when we have a true intuition, it is the intuition of the one and of the identity of the one. For Heraclitus, the fundamental concept relates to difference. It relates to difference because everything which exists becomes constantly different from itself. The third orientation proposed a sort of relationship between identity and difference.

All of that constitutes a general horizon for the philosophical study of the question of change. I propose that at the ontological level of earth we must separate the question of change from the question of multiplicity. My proposal is to produce a division between these two ideas which are actually on the same side. Multiplicity and change are on the side of Heraclitus, and, naturally, it is not possible to think change without thinking the multiple because change is a change from something to something else. If something changes from something to something else then we have multiplicity. If you want to think change you must admit multiplicity, but is the reverse true? That is my point of departure. If you have multiplicity is it a necessity to have change? This is the point, because we can in fact have multiplicity without change. It is possible. This was the primitive intuition of Heraclitus.

Democritus proposed that being is composed of atoms. By itself, an atom is the one, the small one. We have the one in the atom, but the universe is composed of a multiplicity and an infinite amount of atoms. After that we have a change. But this change is a problem because an atom is not by itself in the change. Atoms are practically little Parmenidean beings. Democritus discovered something that was a sort of atomic explosion of what Parmenides discovered. The one is completely destroyed and decomposed into into a multiplicity of very small particles which can not be reduced because each atom is exactly similar to the one of Parmenides. They are small compositions of the world. At the very beginning we also have an orientation which claims that there is no direct relationship between multiplicity and change from the direction of multiplicity toward change.

There is a necessity to the relationship between change and multiplicity. But the reverse, between multiplicity and change, is not a necessity. And it was the obscure intuition of Democritus that, contrary to the idea of Parmenides, we can have multiplicity without change. So it is my contention that being as such is not the one but the multiple. Being as such is pure multiplicity. The point is to affirm that being as such is the multiple as such, and that this multiplicity is by itself not submitted to change. We have a sort of Parmenidean orientation but in the field of multiplicity and not in the field of the one. At the ontological level, I can not assume the consequence of Parmenides' position, that change is a pure illusion. Not at all, I am convinced that change exists, naturally. So I must explain the change.

My position is that the change is not in fact on the side of ontological multiplicity but on the side of the relationship between some multiples. So the change is a relational determination and not a purely ontological determination. There exists relations between some levels only in the particular world. So change is not a property of being as such, change is a property of being when being is localized in a world. You know, change is not the destiny of being as in Heraclitus, but change is a possibility for being when being is localized, inscribed, in a particular world and submitted to some relations with other multiples. Change is an effect of the co-presence of some multiples in the same world, because if they are in the same world they have relations between them, and the field of relations must be a field of change. We can say something like the following: with Heraclitus, I affirm that being *qua* being is not the one but is by itself composed of multiplicities. I can affirm with Heraclitus that being is by itself composed of multiplicity. Against Parmenides, and also against Aristotle, I affirm that the one does not exist. If being is composed of multiplicities, we can not have the one as such. So the one does not exist. It does not exist as a big totality, as in Parmenides, nor as a separated being.

The first movement is on the side of Heraclitus. It is the negation of the one as a big closed totality, it is the negation of the one as a separated being not submitted to change, and so on. After that, I affirm with Parmenides that being itself is not by necessity submitted to change. Pure multiplicity must be thought without any vision of a change. The world of being *qua* being, the world of ontology, is composed of multiplicity, but this world is by itself motionless. The point is that a multiple can not be called another multiple at the ontological level. I will explain why momentarily, but a multiple is absolutely different from another multiple. If the difference is absolute then we can not have the transformation of the first multiple into another multiple.

The ontological world is composed of multiplicities which all have their proper identities, and their identities can not change at the natural level. So I agree with Parmenides that being is not moved. That is the general vision. There is something from the Heraclitian position, something from the Parmenidean position, and, in fact, nothing coming from the visions of Aristotle or Kant. In fact, Aristotle and Kant are my philosophical enemies [laughter]. Okay, so I gave some credit to Parmenides and I gave some credit to Heraclitus, but this does not mean that I claim the sort of division we have seen with Aristotle's concept of god, where there is a part of being not submitted to change that is the cause of all everything which exists. The difficult question is: how can I think the multiple as such? How is it possible to have rational access to the world of pure multiplicity without change? After all, maybe Kant is correct. Maybe I can affirm by pure faith that being is composed of multiplicity.

My pure hypothesis is that the being of pure possibility is composed of multiplicity. It is possible to have a conversation about this proposition, it is possible to complete Kant by claiming that being as such is probably composed of multiplicity. But I don't know, it is probably a faith, it is something like a hypothesis. My answer to the problem of how I can think the multiple as such – pure multiplicity, without any qualitative determination, without any change – is that I can know it through mathematics. Not only is it a possibility, but it is a scientific possibility. Ontology can be reduced to mathematics under the idea that being as such is composed of pure multiplicity.

Historically, this point became clear at the end of the nineteenth century with the creation of the theory of sets by [Georg] Cantor. Soon after, practically all of mathematics was exposed to the language of set-theory. All of mathematics could be reduced to a notion inside of the theory of sets. In some sense, the theory of sets became the pure theory of the multiple as such. Finally, we can say that all of mathematics was the historical development of the thinking of multiplicity.

Cantor gave us a new means for thinking mathematics as the thinking of multiplicity. The conclusion is very simple: ontology is mathematics. We can finally understand a very mysterious question: why does mathematics give us a way to understand the laws of the world? Einstein claimed that it was something like a miracle. Why did the appropriation of mathematics, which is a pure abstract construction and pure rationality created by the Greeks, without any concrete goal, allow us to begin to understand the complete world? Why is there a pure and miraculous relationship between this pure creation of the human mind [mathematics] and the objective reality of the world? If mathematics is in fact a true thinking of being as such then the question is not really obscure. With mathematics, we have the possibility of understanding the real in its ontological determination.

Being as such is not something mysterious, something hidden, and something that we can not understand. Being as such is composed of pure multiplicities, revealed to us by mathematics. At the ontological level we can have a complete opposition. Being as such is composed of multiplicities. The one does not exist, and god does not exist. We can think rationally about pure multiplicities through mathematics as the true ontology. But mathematics is an ontology in development because it is a science, and science is in development. The point is that, finally, ontology is not a philosophical discipline. It is a scientific discipline.

We must now examine the question of change, because we know that mathematics is not a science of change. Physics was created by mathematical means but also with something else, which is experience. Experience, in physics, is the appropriation of mathematics to the question of change. But by itself mathematics does not say anything about change. All of our ideas about change are proposed by experience. If you study mathematics then you can not find any part within mathematics which claims that multiplicity changes. We can have mathematical mechanics, but mathematical mechanics has some experience within itself. It is clear that the question of change can not be solved inside of ontology itself. The point of departure is also very simple: we must examine the question of change through physics.

What is physics? Physics is not the study of being in general, physics is the study of the world. It is the study of our world, the world we know. This is a world which is composed of galaxies, planets, movements, gravitation, and so on. We must admit that physics is not of an ontological nature because it is submitted to an experience. We do not know at all if our world is *the* world. We have the possibility to claim something like that. But in the beginning, the idea was that our planet was the center of the world, and all things were around that world. After that, it was not the case at all, because we discovered that we were a small planet in the corner of the universe without any particularity. We know that we can find other planets anywhere and we know that the universe is composed of many galaxies. We also know that our galaxy has no particularity, it is also in the very corner of the universe, and so on.

And so a part of physics is appropriate to the world, and to the world which is our world or our experience. Naturally, we have new means for our experience today. We have new machines to explore the universe, and these machines are a result of physics. All machines are results of the new physics. But the simple idea is that when we go from mathematics to physics, we also go from a form of abstract universality toward the necessity of experience of a particular world. It is at the level of this experience of a particular world that we have the necessity to think change. It is very interesting to observe the birth of physics in the texts of Galileo, Newton, and so on. Within these texts we can find a passage toward the new forms of mathematics, integral and inferential calculus, and so on. The physical invention is an extraordinary story.

Ontology is the pure thinking of some multiplicities, it is the true thinking of an infinite multiplicity. After that, there is the physical experience, which is the concrete relationship to our world. We can state the question in a different manner: why does a pure multiplicity not change? We must return to the ontological level. A pure multiplicity can not change because a multiple is defined by its elements. Strictly speaking, a multiplicity is a multiplicity of elements. So one multiple is defined by its elements. What is *another* multiplicity? Another multiplicity is a multiplicity with different elements. You know, a multiplicity which is defined by the same elements is the same multiplicity, because there is no other definition of the multiplicity other than one that is a composition of its elements. So we can not say that a multiplicity has the same elements and is different. It is nonsense.

When a multiplicity is different there exists an element of the first multiplicity which is not in the second multiplicity or an elements of the second multiplicity which is not in the first. The difference is of an absolute nature. If only one element is not the same, the multiplicity is different. The first multiplicity can not become the second because to become the second the first would have to have the same elements. But if the multiplicity has different elements, then it is not the same. So it is impossible to have an understanding of a multiplicity becoming another multiplicity. The two different multiplicities are absolutely different and can not be transformed by any ontological process. This is the principle of extensionality.

Extensionality means that the difference is the difference defined by elements. The great ontological principle is extensional. If two multiplicities are different then there exists one element – maybe many more, but one in any case – which is an element of the first and not an element of the second. This is the axiom of extensionality. It is the ontological axiom of the theory of pure multiplicity. If we consider multiplicities as such then we can not have an understanding of change because of the absoluteness of difference. It is only when the difference is relative that we can have a change because when the difference is absolute we can not pass from one term to another term. The question of change is the question of the difference which is relative to the world. It is not a difference which is ontological, like the extensional difference.

We can say it in another manner: we must have qualitative differences and not only quantitative differences. We clearly understand that the principle of extensionality is of quantitative nature. We have an element on one side which is not an element on the other side, and so an element more or an element less. It is quantitative. It is the quantitative composition of multiplicities which describes the difference. If we must think change we must not simplify to this form of difference. When a difference is purely extensional there is no change, and if we have change it is because we have the possibility to think qualitative differences. Something which is red becomes light red, or obscure red. We can understand that something changed.

All of that makes no sense at the ontological level because the ontological level is pure multiplicity. Change is the question concerning the localization of multiplicities in a world, and in a world we have qualitative differences. That is the point. At the level of pure multiplicity we can have something like this:

A

B

Suppose the first multiplicity [A] and the second multiplicity [B]. What signifies that A is not B?

$$(\exists x)\ [(x \in A)\ \text{AND}\ (x \notin B)]$$

There exists an element x which, for example, is an element of A. To claim that A is not the same as B, we must affirm that there exists an element x which is an element of the first and which is not an element of the second. It is not a strange formula, but it is useful for our ontology because we have no experience and so we can only have inscriptions. We have writing, pure writing. It is why mathematics is a formal science. Mathematics is a formal science because it is not the narrative of an experience but rather the inscription of pure multiplicity. Mathematics is by necessity a formal science, and it is formal because it is ontological. It is also why we can claim that ontology is mathematics.

This difference can not be translated as a qualitative difference. It is, properly, the formula of quantitative difference. The most important affirmation concerning change is that when two multiplicities are localized in the same world they can have a qualitative difference. They do not always have a qualitative difference, but they *can* have a qualitative difference. To have a qualitative difference signifies that the difference is intensive and not only extensive. The difference is not reducible to the fact that one element is in the first multiple and not in the second, it is not reducible to quantitative difference or extensional difference. You understand in your experience that there are differences which are not of this world. But there are also differences which are more or less in the qualitative sense, something is more light or more obscure. All of that can not be reduced to the fact that some elements are here [Badiou points to the formula for extensionality, above].

We can have a continuity of differences. Not point by point, not discrete differences, but a continual difference, where there are nuances, and so on. All of that is when we are in the same world, it is when we are in a closed relationship between multiplicities. In a world, there is a complete system of differences. What is a world? It is the complete system of differences between everything that exists within the world. So, a world certainly contains quantitative differences, because in the world we have only multiplicities. The ontological part of the world is multiplicities. In a world, we have that sort of difference. But we have something else, which is a new form of relationship between the multiplicities. It is a very complex relationship between multiplicities which explains the question of change.

We can reduce all of this to a clear point, which is the most delicate and complex point. What is the condition to have qualitative difference? At the ontological level of pure multiplicity there exists only quantitative differences. The thinking about all of that is the job of mathematics. If we are in a world, what is the point? The point is that we have another form of relationship between multiplicities which is the relationship of proximity, similitude, and so on. All of these relationships are qualitative in kind. But what is a qualitative relationship? It is always a relationship of proximity or difference. We can be near something or we can be very far and different from something. It is a question about the identity between two multiplicities. We can write this new relation as follows:

$$id(A,B) = K$$

We can describe this relation as the identity between A and B. It is an identity between two multiplicities. In a world we always have a measure of the identity between two multiplicities. This point is complex and of great importance. When I claim that A and B are in a world, I also claim that A and B are pure multiplicities which conform to the extensional axiom. A and B are in the same part of the world, or A and B are very distant from one another in the world. Or A and B are of the same appearance in the world, or they are very different by their appearance in the world, and so on. I propose to say that the world is always a sort of measure of the identity between two elements of the world; that is, between two multiplicities of the world. In a definite world we always have something like a value of the identity between two multiplicities.

We can say that we are in a world when we know the real identity, the intensity of the identity, between two multiplicities. I want to give an abstract but simple example. Suppose we have a multiplicity which appears in the world of our perception. And suppose that I can say something about the world of our perception. It is a very concrete problem. Suppose we have a multiplicity which appears in the world of our perception in the form of an object. An object is a multiplicity which appears in the world of our perception. A multiplicity becomes an object in the world. So, for example, a multiplicity appears in the form of an object which is round and dark red [(R,dr)]. And suppose there is another object in the world, another multiple, which appears as an object which is square and light blue [(S,lb)]. We have a first object, round and dark red, and the second, square and light blue. The identity between the two from the point of view of our perception is certainly small:

$$id[(R,dr),(S,lb)]$$

The conclusion will be that the identity between the object we have here, round and dark red, and the other object, which is square and light blue, is probably small. They are not really identical, or their identity – if there exists a measure of their identity – is very small. It is clear that there appears an object which is round and light red. This object is much more identical to the object which is round and dark red than it is to the object which is square and light blue.

All of this is to claim that these differences are not extensional. They are all intensive, or qualitative. All of these differences are qualitative and the result is a sort of measure of identity between the objects. It is the identity of appearance in the world of our perception and so it is a qualitative or intensive difference. The general conclusion is simple: a world is first a system of multiplicities, wherein, between these multiplicities there is a relationship of identity which has value. The value is big or small inside of a world as such. You must understand that the relationship between the multiplicities depends on the world. It depends on the measure of identities in the world.

If the identity is very small then we can say that we have a strong qualitative difference. If the identity is very high then we have a true identity. We can have all of the possible degrees between the a strong identity – which is an indiscernible difference, which is the same object in the world – and the complete difference without any relationship between the two. And so we have the construction of a qualitative universe, and inside the qualitative universe we can understand the question concerning change. The change is the change inside the qualitative identities. It is the transformation of the qualitative relation to other multiplicities. The change is always the change inside the measure of identities between some multiplicities.

It is perfectly clear in physics. Physics is always a measure of a modification of contextual identities between some multiplicities. All of that composes a complex but coherent proposition concerning the question of change. We can return to the more philosophical level by a question which is very fascinating. It is the question of a world, because we are inside of a particular world [W] and we have the function or measure of identity:

$$W \qquad id()$$

Can we rationally ask the question of the possibility of the identity of some multiple to itself?

$$W \qquad id(A,A)$$

After all, why not? You know, this question has no signification at the ontological level because a multiple is certainly identical to itself, evidently, because a multiple is defined by its elements. If we have two multiples with the same elements then they are absolutely the same. At the ontological level, the question of the identity of a multiple to itself is solved immediately. Yes, a multiple, ontologically, is identical to itself. It is what we can name the reflexive principle. But in a world this is not the case. There is no rational reason for there to be a pure identity of a multiple to itself as a law. Maybe the appearing of the multiplicity of an object is something like a contradictory proposition. That is, maybe it is something which is not a pure identity onto itself.

As a metaphorical example, I can say that in some circumstances I have the internal experience of not being completely myself. You know, the concrete psychological experience is explained through the common expression "I was not completely myself today." It is the signification that in some circumstances you are not exactly identical to yourself. You can generalize from this experience. It is absolutely possible that in a concrete world some object is not completely identical to itself. This signifies that an object can be not completely in the world. If, in a world, the object is not absolutely identical to itself, then we can recognize from it that there is a part of itself at the ontological level which is not completely in the world. We know perfectly that something can be in the world with all of its strengths but with a weakness of appearing in the world, and so on.

A world is composed of variations of the identity of the thing to itself. It is possible to be in a very violent light in a world, or to be in obscurity in a world, where we can not really see if you are in the world, and so on. These are fundamental examples which have magnificent philosophical consequences. We can suppose that the identity of a multiple to itself in a world is not its ontological identity insofar as this identity to itself has a measure. It is not always true that a thing is absolutely identical to itself, but an object can appear with weakness or with strength, it can be completely in the world or not completely in the world, and so on. So we have a measure of the identity of itself, a measure of the multiple, in the world. This measure of the identity of a multiple to itself in a world we can name existence. It is the existence of the multiple. Here, we have the most important conceptual distinction between existence and being. Being is the ontological identity for an object in a world, it is being as such. The ontological identity is the identity of the multiple, and a multiple is always identical to itself. At this level, there is a clear vision of identity.

If the multiple is in a world then there are immediately many relationships between different multiples; an identity with some, a non-identity with some others, and so on. Inside of this complex measure of identity with other multiplicities there is also a possible modification of the identity to itself. The degree of the identity of a thing to itself in the world is named its existence. I insist on the point that existence is a concept relative to a world. The pure identity of a multiple is not relative to a world, it is its ontological identity. But when the multiple is in a world it can have another form of identity – which is a qualitative identity and which is not of absolute value – which can change its identity to itself. What we have here is the measure of its existence.

Finally, a multiple can exist in a world in different manners. In our concrete experience we know that we can have different forms of identities when we are in different worlds. For example, when we are in a world where we do not know the language, we immediately experience the change of our identity to ourselves. What we know, what we can do, what we can say, and so on, has changed; the language is not even the same. At the ontological level you are the same person, but you exist differently. To be the same and yet to exist in difference is precisely the entire point of change. And so we can clearly understand what it means to change something. The change of something is the change of its existence, but inside of the change of its existence we also have the ontological identity of its being and this can not disappear. It subsists inside the change of existence, it subsists inside the change of your presence in the world.

Existence is not reducible to being. That is the point. And so we can understand why we are simultaneously Parmenidean and Heraclitian. You are Parmenidean insofar as you are always reducible to pure being at the ontological level. Pure being does not change, it is rather submitted to change. A pure multiple, as it is told in mathematics, is the composition of yourself. It is who you are. You are a multiple who can not change. So there really is a Parmenidean level. But at the level of existence, within a particular world, we can have a change of identity itself. This existence shows identity, but it is not ontological identity. And so we can claim that something changed. You know, if something changes it is not the same something, but we can not say that *something* changed. Here, we can say that *A* changed; it is a change of degree for its existence in the world. At one moment it is the measure of an identity and at another moment it is another measure of an identity. Its existence changed. We have the right to claim that because it is the same multiple. The identity of *A* to itself changed but *A* as such does not change.

We have a concrete and coherent answer to the question of change. We have a theory of change which is really also a theory of non-change. It is a necessity, because without that we are purely Heraclitian, and for Heraclitus there is no identity at all. For Heraclitus, change is being and being is change. In a Heraclitian universe, we can not claim that something changed, you can only claim that something becomes something else. There is no permanency to the something which changes. You know, to completely think about change we must have a point which does not change. The point which does not change is the measure of the possibility of change. In that sort of conception we have two levels: we have the level where multiplicity is identical to itself, but we have the other level where something is a relation of the multiple to itself and not the multiple as such. The identity of A and A is a relation of A to A, where a relation of a multiple to itself is submitted to change.

Finally, we can say all of this very clearly: as pure multiplicity, being is not submitted to change. As a multiplicity inscribed in a world, we can claim that its existence is submitted to change. Finally, being is not submitted to change but existence is submitted to change. The reconciliation of ontology and existentialism depends upon the acceptance that existence is the place for change inside of an ontological context. And this ontological is Parmenidean, but without the one. All of that is a consequence of the negation of the one. After that, we can have a vision of change. This vision is expressed through the conceptual difference between being and existence. All of this is for tomorrow. [audience applauds]

A few thoughts on the future of our seminar. We will begin with your questions tomorrow. I have a lot of questions, and they are complex questions. After that we will read the poem from [Paul] Valéry. That will be for the day after tomorrow. You will discover that the poem explains all of the problems of the relationship between being and existence. The great movement of the poem is to begin with being, immobility. And it moves progressively toward a sort of opening of existence.

Day Four

Seminar Six

*Time as such * Inscription * Set & number, Multiplicity & Numericity * Reality, mathematics, and discursivity * Being & time * Getting outside of Plato's cave * Power and change * An idea, a conviction, and an event * Heroism * A lesson from my father*

Good afternoon. I have divided the questions into five themes. First, there are what I name the technical questions. These questions relate to mathematics and so they are only indirectly related to philosophy. Second, there are some questions concerning politics or ethics. Third, there is a question concerning aesthetics. Fourth, there are some important questions concerning life and death. And after that there are questions concerning ecology and the general vision of change. I think I can give an answer to the first categories but the final questions, concerning the general vision of change, I will leave for the end of our seminars. I propose to organize another hour seminar for the end of the week.

I also have given you a second translation of the poem by Paul Valéry. It will be interesting for you to examine not only the text itself but also the difference between the two translations. It is symptomatic. Maybe it is not even the same text at all. And so it is interesting that this is a radical change in the form of a translation of a poem from one language to another language. It may be an example of a change. What exactly is the poem as such, the being of the poem? It is a very interesting question.

I will begin with a technical question. You can read the question.

Student: Can change be mapped or diagrammed mathematically? How is mathematics related to ontology, as inconsistent multiplicity, in such a way that being is not simply reduced to or conflated with number, since in your own terms the one is not? Your position seems to imply that the Pythagorean identification of being and number is precluded in advance. Furthermore, how is it that the set theoretical axiomatization of being, exemplified through the operation of the count-as-one which produces consistent multiplicity from inconsistent multiplicity, be said to secure a connection with extra-discursive reality?

Badiou: I think that it is a very interesting question. My first answer is to propose that our problem concerns having a rational knowledge of change. The expressions from Deleuze are in fact of a spatial nature insofar as they carried the idea of a spatial representation of change. The question for Deleuze was about how change is fundamentally a matter relating of time. If you propose a spatial presentation of change then you have something which is really a change of change because it is a passage from time to space. It is a classical question within philosophy and it relates to the vitalist orientation. It is something which is within the paradigm of the philosophy of life. A philosophy of life is always also a philosophy of time because the true becoming of life is within time.

When Deleuze, and his master on this point Henri Bergson, asked the question of change it was essentially the question of spatial time. Bergson distinguished between the time of life or creation and the time of physics. These two times were not the same. It is a question of spatial time. It is always a difficult problem because we must project time into a spatial image or spatial representation. It is why your question is in some sense a Deleuzian or Bergsonian question, or, finally, a Heraclitian question. Everything is in time because everything is change. So, in some sense, being is time. *Sein* is time. I agree completely with the formulation of the problem. If being as such is identified with the movement of time then the real question is, how can we give a spatial image of change as such? For example, Bergson claimed that mathematical time – that is, time in classical physics – is not real time. It is not the real time of life but is a sort of image of time, a spatial image of time.

It is a very important discussion about how we can think time as such. We can begin another seminar on the question of time. It would be interesting because the question of time is very close to the question of change. Maybe, in some sense, this was the idea of Aristotle. Maybe time is only an abstract representation of change. If we are close to the Heraclitian idea that being is change, or that being is becoming, as you've written in your question [note: the seminar group only had access to the oral presentation of the question and not the written question] then we have a very difficult question concerning the thinking of time as such. The projection of time as an image, or the question of time in symbols, is not completely adequate to the immanent strength of time.

We can admit that we have the possibility of having a rational knowledge of time, a knowledge which is marked or diagrammed. For example, the representation of change is mathematical symbolism. The point is that mathematical symbolism, and symbolic activity more generally, is neither temporal nor spatial. It is not spatial because it is not an image. It is not a spatial presentation of change. It is something like an inscription. But an inscription is not space proper and it is not time. Symbolic activity, which is characteristic of human beings, is neither temporal nor exactly spatial. We can name it something like an inscription or we can claim that it is something literal, something of the letter. This is a very old idea. The letter is not empirical in nature.

If we assume that being as such is not identical to change then in some sense being as such is not submitted to change. There is a sort of symbolism which is adequate to inscribe being. If we represent being by something temporal or spatial then we represent being as submitted to change. To think change as such we must think something like the being of change, and so it is not surprising that the science of change is semiotic in nature. My conviction is that this is why physics has been written in mathematical language. It was the rustic affirmation of Galileo to claim that nature is written in mathematical language. I think that this is not actually true. It is not nature, exactly, which is written in mathematical language because being is not reducible to nature. Nature is something like being with the idea of a world. So nature, in general, refers to being localized within a world. But for Galileo, nature was a name for being as such. Nature was the being of being and so nature was written in mathematical language. That relates to the first part of your question.

For the second part of the question I would like to resume with the following idea: if being is written in mathematical language then we return to the idea that being is number, that being is made of numbers, and that there is a numerical reality of being. This was the idea of Pythagoras, it was that, effectively, nature was numbers. On this point, it is very important to distinguish between a set and a number. When we say that we think being in the form of a mathematical framework of sets we are not saying that being is therefore reducible to number. I have written a book about this question called *Number and Numbers* [cf., Polity Press, 2008]. I explain at the beginning of the book that Cantor's theory of sets teaches us that there is a difference between multiplicity and numericity. Some multiplicities are numbers, but many multiplicities are not numbers. The concept of a set is more vast than the concept of a number, a number is only a small part of the general existence of pure multiplicity. And so I am not Pythagorean.

In passing, you have claimed in your own terms that when I say "the one is not" I am inviting a Pythagorean identification of being with number which is precluded in advance. I think this credit for me is unjust [laughter]. First, it is not at all Pythagoras's idea that the one is not. On the contrary, the basis of all Pythagorean mathematics is that the one *is*, and that it *is* fundamentally the first term of the theory of numbers. For Pythagoras, all numbers which are natural numbers are necessarily composed of the one. Two is two ones, three is three ones, and so on. Not only does the one exist for Pythagoras, and more generally for the Greek arithmetic, but the one is the culmination of numericity. In some sense we learn this also today: one, two, three, four, all of these are composed by ones. Two is one and one, three is one and one and one, and so on. So, it is the continuation and proliferation of the one, which is number.

It is why there was a great revolution in arithmetics with the invention of Zero. Zero is completely absent in Greek arithmetic. The zero was an Arabic invention. This is of fundamental importance because it was a revolution in thinking. The basis of thinking in the Greek framework was the one. Not only in mathematics but in all dimensions of Greek philosophy. It was not necessarily always the big one of Parmenides, but some form of the one was always there at the beginning of thinking. When I claim that the one does not exist it is only to claim that we have multiplicity without the one, or that the multiplicity is not composed of the one. And multiplicity in the theory of sets is composed of the void. The beginning is not the one, it is the zero. So I am more Arabic than Greek.

On the contrary, for your question – but it is still a good question – we can claim that the Pythagorean orientation, which was that the world is mathematical in nature, was a great orientation in some sense. But this idea was absolutely reduced to the fact that mathematics signifies natural numbers. Finally, we have the position that the world is composed of numbers. It is difficult to assume this point. Maybe the world is composed of mathematics, but this mathematics is not reducible to classical arithmetic.

You made an interesting claim at the end of your question. If we think being across the axiomatization of set-theory, or if we think being through the abstract theory of multiplicities in the mathematical form of set-theory, then how can we have access to being which is not discursive? This has often been an objection against my work, and so it is an objection that I understand. For example, what is the relationship between this glass and the theory of sets? Perhaps there is something which is not reducible to a pure multiple with qualitative dimensions, perhaps there is something completely different insofar as it is natural, and so on. You are claiming that non-discursive reality exists and that this reality is not reducible to the discursivity of mathematics. And then you are asking how we can claim that there is a thinking of being as such. I insist on my answer. It is very important. There is something which is ontological in nature, something which is at the level of being as such, and there is something which is neither spatial nor temporal because time and space are characteristics of a particular world.

In a particular world we have objects like the glass. But these objects are relative to the world itself. Naturally, it is an empirical object which is not completely at the ontological level. So the question of being is not reducible to the spatial-temporal existence of the glass. It is something different. We must admit that, at the ontological level, we have no temporal or spatial characteristics. We have only something which is hidden by the empirical determination. At this level, we absolutely can not think empirically about the object because there is no empirical reference with time and space. It is only the pure inscription which is adequate for thinking the object in its ontological dimension. It is the pure symbol as such. In some sense, we could put this in Heideggerian terms. We have no knowledge of being, we only have a thinking about being.

Okay, so we have no empirical knowledge of being as such, we only have thinking. The only thing reducible to thinking being as such is mathematics. Everything which is not mathematical is empirical, in some sense. If you have a political idea or a geographical idea then there is always an associated experience. But in mathematics there is no experience at all, there are only axioms. Axioms are decisions within thinking, and consequences of these decisions. Mathematics is a form of thinking which not only requires some primitive abstract decisions which are named axioms but it also requires the logical context which determines its consequences. All of this is adequate for a thinking of pure being, and nothing else.

This is why I agree with you when you claim that reality is extra-discursive. I admit that there exists an extra-discursive reality. It is being when being is localized in a particular world, when a multiplicity appears in some world. To think multiplicity as an appearance inside of a world we must have an experience which is not reducible to discourse. It is only if we want the size of the thing, without its appearance, and without its concrete determination in a world, can we have being as such. Thank you for your very precise and interesting question.

The next questions are also very precise and technical, thank you.

Student: You mentioned that change is not the property of being as such but of being when it is localized in a world. So, in this sense, I think you are referring to a power set. The obvious problem is that the power set belongs to sets which are multiplicities in themselves. Since we have no defined idea of what a power set is in itself then we have no way of generating such a set. Since the multiple paradoxically is defined by its elements then we have no way for there to be a set of all of them. What is the solution to this problem both mathematically and philosophically?

Badiou: This is a critique of circular thinking. You say that I claim that being as such is finally representable as a set, but to provide the space of all sets in a change I am obliged to go to the power set of the set. The power set is inside of the theory of sets and this therefore is a circle. The question is about how we can pass from pure sets into a world. What is a world in relation to a theory of sets? Your propose to move from a set to something bigger which we can call the power set. This is not the case at all. A space for all sets in a world is not a power set, it is something else which in the modern mathematical context we name a category. It is not a set, it is a category.

A category is something like a form of mathematical universe, but it is only a metaphor. It is composed of relations between sets rather than being composed purely of sets. The definition is mathematically precise. If you are interested in the technical discussion of this point you can find the complete solution to your problem in my *Logics of Worlds* [Continuum, 2009; Trans. Alberto Toscano]. We must insist on the point that change is not directly a question of sets in the universe, rather it is a question of the relations between sets. Change is always a change of some relation and not a change of the set itself. There is no change of the set itself. A set is what it is and can not change, but the relation between two differences can change. We can affirm that we can have change in a world because we have relationships between differences in a world. How all of this works is explained in complex form in *Logics of Worlds*. You can read it in simpler form in the *Second Manifesto for Philosophy* [Polity Press, 2011]. After our seminar, it will certainly be useful for you to read the *Second Manifesto*.

I insist on the point that the concept of change is relative in two senses. First, change is relative to a world. We can not speak of a change without specifying within what world we observe the change. It is a clear rule of physics that there is always a determination of the context and scale of the phenomenon. For example, the world of micro-physics is not the same world as the world of macro-physics. They are not based on the same law. Second, change is a question of a change of relations between sets or beings. We can claim that a change is always the change of the value of an identity between two (or many) sets. If we have two beings inscribed in a world then we also have a measure of the identity between the two points. A relation between two points is also a relation of identity. A change in the world [W] is a change of the identity of X and Y.

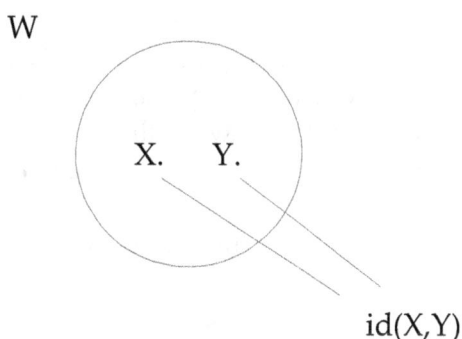

W

X.   Y.

id(X,Y)

It is very simple. A measure of identity can be a measure which is big or small, and we can have a change because we have a change of the intensional relation between sets.

We can also have a change of the identity of something to itself. It is a change of the relation of X to itself. This is a change of existence. The existence of the set is different from its being. Its being is always absolutely identical to itself, but its existence in a concrete world can not always be absolutely identical to itself. We perfectly know in our experience that sometimes we have a strong identity to ourselves and sometimes we do not. In any case, abstraction is the inscription of the concept.

Your second question?

Student: In *Difference & Repetition,* Deleuze informs us that unity must be understood as a secondary operation, under which difference is pressed into forms. Deleuze was paraphrasing Nietzsche by claiming that being is becoming. The prominent philosophical notion that he offers for such a unity is time. So, the solution is, to put it in Heideggerian terms, that what unites all of the different modes of being is that they realize some form of presentness. I'm asking if you agree with this or not. And, how can we put this into set-theory?

Badiou: Naturally, I do not agree [laughter]. I do not agree because that is only true if being is becoming. If being is becoming then unification is a question of time. And the unification of being in time is a very difficult question. It is a question of presence, whereby the thing is itself in the current time. This is its pure presentness. You can have the recollection of the composition of the thing because this composition is in fact created in time. So you have a pure change of the thing and the possibility to speak of an identity of the thing by cutting time. But what is the current of time? It is pure presence. So it is about being identified only if they are of the same presentness, only if they are absolutely co-present. All of this is perfectly coherent. It is the Heraclitian choice. Being is becoming and becoming is change, and so on.

We have returned to the great problem of the question of time. It is true that, with Heraclitus, we can claim that time is a child's game. This is the magnificent formula from Heraclitus, time is the game of a child. After that, we can not understand anything because if time is becoming itself then there is no thinking of what is in time. Time is naive and obscure, and it is the game of a child. For a true Heraclitian, being as such is time itself and it is the game of a child. If you assume the identity between being and becoming then you must have the idea that unity comes after, through a cut in time, as the current presentness.

After many years of meditation, this eventually became the Deleuzian conception of the plane. There is the philosophical plane, the scientific plane, and the artistic plane, and all of these planes capture the size of things in different ways with regard to the general becoming. They are cuts in becoming. And the plane is the plane where the thing is inscribed in its presentness.

Thank you for all of those very interesting questions. We turn now to questions concerning politics and ethics.

Student: The question concerns organizational coercion and change. When a subject is situated within institutions that ask for a professional and *de facto* silence, at what point could one be seen as working on the outside when one is immobilized like this? What type of position does one have to have to decide this?

Badiou: It is a very difficult question. In the end, it is what I have named a topological question. It is a question about the outside and the inside and the different situations of thinking and of action. The problem is that there is a difficulty to completely understand this point because, in some sense, we are always inside. We are inside institutions and countries, and many other determinations. We know perfectly that we are also inside many oppressive situations and that these create immobility and silence, so that we will stay inside. All of that is true. When you say that a subject is situated within institutions which ask for professionalism and *de facto* silence, we can call that a sort of experience. So what must compose the movement from inside to outside?

To be outside means that we must be open to new possibilities outside of the state and outside of institutions, and so on. I think all of you know the allegory of the cave from Plato. It is exactly the problem of Plato. Plato claimed that all human beings are enclosed in a cave. In this cave we can not see any truth, we only see appearances, shadows, which are separated from truth. To open the possibility of truth we must go outside. This is why Plato claimed something like what you have claimed: everybody is situated within institutions where immobility and silence are forms of negation. Plato wanted to open up access to truth in order to become a real subject rather than just a prisoner. In this case, human beings are prisoners of appearances. To become a subject we must go outside. In fact, it was the same central question: how can we go outside? And how can we decide to go outside? If we are inside then how is it possible to go outside? And what can be decided on this point?

This is why the allegory of the cave is so famous and so important. It is really the central problem of the emancipation of human kind. If the determination is absolute, if to be inside is to be under absolute law in the absurd and criminal sense, then we can not have any hope to go outside. If life is always on the inside then to push people to go outside may perhaps be to push them to death. It is why we have many arguments from those in power that "reality is such and such, and you can not change reality." They claim that "you can not change, you can not go outside." The fundamental propaganda of power is the claim that we must stay inside because it is rational, reasonable and necessary to stay inside. In other words, it is because it is the reality. So, the problem of the cave, which is the problem of the Platonist, is a real problem.

I can say a few words concerning the possibility of this possibility to go outside. My claim is that we must begin with the idea that power, the state, and the institutions of power, are on the inside of the cave. All of these are in a closed relationship to change. But the inside is not indifferent to the question of change. Power does not claim: "No change at all!" Very often, power screams "Change, Change, Change, We Need Change!" "We are conservative! Be the change! Be active, transform the world!" There is a very close relationship between power and change, there is not a pure contradiction between the two. The key to answering the question of power is not to describe it as tradition as such. Very often we have the idea that power is the incarnation of immobility and of tradition. Not at all. Tradition is a subjective interpretation of the different determinations of power as such. There can exist traditional power but there can also exist revolutionary power. Power as such is the determination of what is possible. Power has a strong relation to change because it articulates what change is really possible.

So, power can be defined according to this potency of articulating what sort of change is possible and what sort of change is impossible. Naturally, power claims that if a change is possible then it is good and if a change is impossible then it is bad. If we read the propaganda of every power, it would demonstrate this point; "We want change, we love change," claims power. "We want reforms, many reforms of everything that exists." And very often power claims: "I am for change, it is the people who are conservative!" It is because the question of power is not the question of change, rather the question of power is a question of the determination of possible change. Possible change is change which is compatible with power. It is not that change is forbidden but that power defines what is the correct change.

We must propose a true definition of what it is to be inside. Naturally, to be inside can first of all mean that we are inside of an objective situation. That is, it could mean that we are compelled to do something. I am not claiming that power is never oppressive and violent. That is absolutely possible. But to be inside is also a subjective situation. It is not only to be compelled to do something but also to accept that the state, or power more generally, decides the possibilities concerning what constitutes good change. It is not really to forbid change. Finally, it is also the subjective conviction that it is the state which decides the possibilities. The first steps in the direction of the outside are made by knowing, thinking, and becoming convinced that it is not true that the state holds the key to all possibilities. This is the first rupture with the state and with the inside because we are generally compelled to do something after first accepting the fundamental fact that the state decides the possibilities. There is something much more immediate which is the subjective rupture with the conviction, which is very often our own everyday conviction, that power decides the possibilities for change.

The first step is to know and to have the real conviction that it is not true that the state decides the possibilities. We are at the level of an idea. It is a subjective determination which is not immediately active but which is nonetheless real. It is a concrete subjective conviction that it is not true that power, institutions, and so on, decide all of the possibilities. This is the first step toward the outside. I name this step an idea. It is the idea of something else, it is the very idea of an outside. But it is not the idea of an outside as a purely abstract idea, but rather it is the idea of an outside as the place where we can define possibility in another manner. It is the place where new possibilities exist. And these are not reducible to the state because we know that it is not true that the state decides all possibilities. Maybe something which is impossible is really possible. It is why there is always a struggle from power against this sort of idea. This idea is considered utopian, or it is considered a terrorist idea. And it is a simple idea that the general state of affairs does not decide all possibilities.

At its very beginning, communism was explicitly this sort of idea. The idea was that there could be a world not organized by private property. All of the propaganda claimed that man was absolutely linked to property. And today too. So, you know, there is this subjective step between the inside and the outside. I think there are three terms, not two. The first term is the subjective conviction. This is certainly something inside, but it is a movement. It is the subjective movement in the direction of the outside. This is exactly why Plato spoke about ideas. For the prisoner of the cave to go outside there was a necessity of the position to go outside. At the beginning, we are all prisoners in the cave. We see nothing, everything is obscure. There is a master of the cave who claims that everything is perfect. We must create something in the dark, we must go across appearing. It is exactly our situation. And so Plato claimed that we can go outside of the cave if we have something like an idea. You must change your subjectivity first, you must create something like a subjectivity of the outside, a subjectivity without an inside.

To properly be outside, we must have the idea of the new possibility, but also something more. We need something more. We need to find the means to realize the path of beginning this possibility. Naturally, we must have some help from an event. Something happens which is adequate to the idea. Something happens that we can not calculate or organize because it is something which happens by change. It is something which occurs as a dysfunction of the inside. The inside is not exactly good or the master of the cave is ill [laughter]. There is some trouble with the master. In the light, we see something in the master. All of that would be an event. You know that it is event, but why? Maybe, it is only a sort of accident, a sort of pathology of the cave or a pathology of the inside. But it becomes an event because we have the idea, and the idea is the reception of the event in the direction of the outside and not only through catastrophic meditation.

There is propaganda concerning the idea of crisis today. Today, a crisis is something which is good for the inside. It is not very good because it means that there is no work, there is a financial disaster, and so on. If we can transform all of that into a positive event then it is only because we have an idea of the outside. If we stay within the idea of the inside then we are with the government and we are basically saying to the public that there is a crisis but you must be inside and, in fact, we must be more inside than ever before. The lesson from the government during a crisis is to be absolutely and energetically inside. They claim that we must work harder and that the coming years will be very difficult for us, but after that the inside will be even more miraculous.

Finally, my answer to the question about who decides is that it is everybody, because we must have a change of the subjective relationship to the inside. We can not decide about the subjective relationship toward the inside, it is the individuals themselves who decide through the function of the idea. It is their experience of possibility. So, you know, this question is very interesting. It is a new interpretation of change. You know, I think that we have two different changes in a concrete situation. We have the change inside of the inside, which is a subjective change concerning the possibilities of the inside. It is the displacement of the center of possibilities, which is by definition the law of the inside. If we displace the center of possibilities then we have the possibility for a collective idea, and so we have the disposition required to accept the position that we must go outside. Our disposition is that to go outside is not something catastrophic, or that it is a positive catastrophe.

That is an answer to the first and important question. Now, we have another question from a student.

Student: It is not so complicated. I would like to know why you claimed that this is not a time for heroes. Thank you.

Badiou: It is a question about heroism. In my lectures, I have said that many philosophers today – and perhaps it is even the dominant opinion – claim that our time is not the time for heroes. Heroism is a form of subjectivity, it is a possible qualitative dimension of subjectivity which goes beyond private interests on behalf of an idea. This is a very general definition of heroism, at any period of history. A subject who accepts heroism is a subject with the conviction that in some circumstances the value of existence, the science of existence, can be measured by the fidelity to an idea.

I insist that heroism can not be a blind conviction or a desire for sacrifice. We know that the obstinacy for the taste of sacrifice is something different from heroism. Heroism is not a negative determination, it is a rational conviction that in some circumstances, but not always, we must act on behalf of an idea and not according to our pure interests. True heroism is rational, it is not a passion without determination. The affirmation of an idea is not madness, and it is not pure glory. It is an intimate conviction, but it can be discussed and examined, and the hero can be convinced by rational argumentation. This is why heroism is a very important part of literature and art. Maybe the question of the hero is the first form of great artistic narrative, because the figure of the hero is something like the practical existence of an idea. It is not the abstract existence of an idea, but rather the personal and subjective existence of an idea. Naturally, heroism must be discussed as a rational signification and not as some sort of madness, desire of negativity, desire for sacrifice, or, finally, the Freudian death drive.

You question is a good one because today's dominant ideology recognizes that subjective desire is reduced to happiness, a good life, satisfaction, money, and so on. And the subject is saving in order to discovery its harmony. But heroism is not harmony. It is rational, but it is not harmony because it is the acceptance of the idea that the measure of life is in some sense outside life itself. It is an idea that is a component of the world, but it is not directly reducible to the practical existence of the hero. In some sense, the point is that, for the hero, life is not the supreme value. You know, very often heroism involves exposing yourself to the possibility of death for the conviction of an idea. But this is not the definition of heroism. Naturally, the hero can accept that in some circumstances his or her life must be made vulnerable for the idea. But this is the limit of heroism and not its definition. The definition is only that the value of existence, and so the value of life, is in some circumstances determined by the fidelity to an idea.

You can learn from my experience. My father was in the resistance against the Nazis during the last great war. I often said to my father, "but why?" It was a terrible experience. There was not only death, but also torture and suffering. It was terrible. My father responded, and he was absolutely rational – he was, after all, a professor of mathematics [laughter], and not a militant: "yes, it was difficult; but my conviction was that in these circumstances, with the German Nazis occupying my country, I must absolutely resist. I can accept that." It can be at the price of my life. But the fact that it is at the price of my life is not the subjective definition of that sort of common heroism. It was simply the rational conviction that the idea of the emancipation of people against fascism, against the Nazis, was a measure of the value of existence. And he said to me – it was the lesson of my father – that if he did not do this, then it would all be something like zero. It would be a value of zero if he was not in existence.

The point for today is that in some circumstances the value of life is not in life itself. Heroism is not only about the value of a good life because the life of resistance is very difficult. So maybe you sacrifice your life but it is not a necessity, it is not a definition. But it is a possibility, because the value of life can not stay within life itself. That is the idea. An idea is not reducible to your proper or pre-made life. The point is that, in the capitalist world, there is no idea. There are no other ideas than the ideas of personal happiness, the good life, collective freedom, the right to say what I think, and so on. Nothing of this has the measure of an idea. It is purely the measure of life itself. It is about finding personal harmony within life.

The central contradiction is not between the value of life in the idea and the value of life in life. Today's dominant contradiction is between the good life and suffering. A contradiction between the good life and suffering exists, it is a reality. But it is not a heroic contradiction. It is a defensive contradiction. And it is why I think that the dominant imperative of our society is absolutely not heroic. It is the belief that it is much better to live without any idea because an idea is very often a way for suffering.

This is demonstrated clearly in our society. You know, it was also the question of Plato. In Plato's time, many people were claiming that happiness was the value of existence. But happiness has nothing to do with an idea, it is not in a relationship with an idea. There are many texts from Plato which are proofs of this. Plato's idea was a proof of the contrary. It is the hero who is really and profoundly happy. The hero has the experience of true happiness and not of ordinary happiness. There exists ordinary happiness. Plato does not negate the existence of personal harmony, *jouissance* of power, and so on. But there is a form of happiness which is beyond all of that.

And it was also the idea of my father. My father was not at all a philosopher. Plato was not his master. But he has said that the four years of resistance was certainly the most dangerous and the most critical years of his life. But they were also the happiest years of his life. So, I replied to my father: "Father, you are a good Platonist" [laughter]. Thank you father.

[Applause]

Seminar Seven

*Public, collective, generic, universal * The immanent nothingness of the Proletariat * Neither beyond nor before differences * Art & technology * The architect's compromise * The dialectics of life and death * Civilization as the symbolization of death * Capitalism and the death of god*

We have a system of questions concerning aesthetics.

Student: I have four basic questions regarding aesthetics. Is there a difference in practice of both forms of change according to the following concepts: universal, collective, generic, and public? Where does the aesthetic fall relative to the four orientations on change? Does the aesthetic not privilege the existential through ideas of prosthesis? Can you point to a change in the visual arts in a form that is not linked to a change in technology? And, poetry, theatre, painting, and sculpture, are one thing, but what about architecture?

Badiou: Thank you. The question is in four parts, but it is a coherent question overall. We can understand the question as follows: is aesthetics in the same relationship to truth as something else? Is there a specificity to aesthetics and to the arts regarding the question concerning change?

Regarding the first question, I think we can distinguish the four terms: public, collective, generic, and universal. They are all different. So this is an occasion to be precise about these points. A public is in some sense purely objective. There either exists a public or there does not exist a public. More generally, something is public when it is not enclosed in a private situation, or when something is exposed to everybody. I think that a public is an empirical determination. In fact, there is a particular question of the public for a work of art.

For example, nobody asks for a public for scientific creation. Is there a public for mathematics? In fact, no [laughter]. Mathematicians are very happy to be within their small aristocratic community. Generally, mathematicians are of the opinion that nobody understands anything in mathematics, that is, nobody but themselves understand mathematics. And so they can discuss mathematics with their friends in a closed room. It is not the case for great mathematicians like [Jules Henri] Poincaré or [Leonhard] Euler, but it is the case for many mathematicians. I am absolutely against this disposition and I fight against it. I claim that mathematics is very important for the general understanding of everything that exists. It is the subject of this seminar: all objects of our environment are something like a material concentrate of mathematics. If we admit that mathematics is something completely separate, something aristocratic that the rest of us can not understand, then we have a problem. It is necessary to democratize mathematics. It is difficult, but it is necessary.

Concerning the work of art, we have the question of the public. There is a relationship between the work of art and something which is public. Only some mystic avant-gardes, some esoteric poets, and some abstract painters, are like the mathematicians. They have a very small public. But, generally speaking, the work of art is addressed to a public. The empirical existence of the public is the real question for the work of art itself.

A collective is also in some sense purely objective. Something which is collective is by its very nature composed of many individuals. It is a collective of a multiplicity of individuals. For example, in the field of aesthetics and artistic creation, we can say that some forms of music or theatre are collective. There is some part of art which is collective. Theatre itself is largely collective insofar as it is largely a collective creation. We can not claim that there is only one man and that he owns the only form of theatre. It is an objective determination, but it is not identical to a public because a public is collective and not everything which is collective is a public. For example, we can have collective political action. But collective political action is not exactly public. It is something else.

That which is universal is formal. We give the name universal to everything which has value for every subject, independent of particularities. Something is universal if its value is independent of the particularities of the subject. It is why that which is universal can be reduced to a purely logical expression. You know, it is a question of quantification. There is a symbol of universality:

$$\forall x$$

For all x it is true … And so universality is formal. It is a quality of judgment. It is a question of logical universality. It is neither objective nor subjective, but rather formal. It is the difference between public and collective.

Generic is also objective in some sense because a generic set is a set without the exclusion of differences. It is a set which is not composed of an identity but which is composed of differences and which does not exclude differences. It is the objective composition of the set which is not constructable. That is, it accepts differences inside of its composition. In a concrete situation the generic is also a subjective determination because a generic set is constructed by accepting a common truth. And a common truth is common to all differences. The generic is not only a formal universality with differences but it is also a subjective position. In politics, it is clear. The vision of genericity is a one which goes beyond nationalism, racism, and so on. The generic is always something which is the construction of a collectivity as a representation of humanity as such. It is the acceptance of all forms of positive differences.

I recall that Marx claimed that the proletariat was the name for generic humanity. It is interesting in the context of my lecture because it is fundamentally a question of negativity. Marx affirmed the generic dimension of the working class as nothing. The working class was nothing. But if, in a world which is defined by private property, you have nothing, then you are nothing. In some sense, the proletariat is the name for the void within bourgeois society. It is the name of the empty set or the name of the nothing. We are nothing, we are the international, we recognize these points. But it is a metaphysical or ontological determination. And it has a relationship to the generic. Generic is nothing that has no identity. If we claim that to be somebody we must have an identity, then, for Marx, the proletariat was nothing because it has no proper identity. It is composed of individuals with nothing but their body and their work. But they have nothing. In the Bourgeois society, they are nothing because they have nothing.

So for Marx there was a relationship between the generic and nothingness. It is the fundamental reason for the relationship between Marx and Hegelian dialectics. First there is being, which is bourgeois society. Next, there is the immanent nothingness of being, which is the proletariat. And after that we have the becoming of revolution. This is the general framework. All across society people are defined as something by private property. And then there are those with the nothingness of this being, who do not own property, whom are named the proletariat. The movement of the two is the political movement of revolution. And then we have a society without class, without any private property.

Marx wrote in his manifesto that the communist program can be summed up in one sentence: the abolition of private property. It is the abolition of being, by the active nothingness of the proletariat, with respect to the society. I do not completely assume the Marxist position on this point because I believe that it is very dangerous to define genericity by nothingness. It is a fundamental discussion, and not at all an abstract discussion. Perhaps the question for politics today is to substitute the negative definition of genericity with a positive one. We can affirm that genericity is really a complexity of differences rather than the pure absence of being. Marx claimed this as the truth when he wrote that to be a communist is also to be an internationalist. To claim that communism is internationalism is to also recognize that there is something different from the pure nothingness of the proletariat. We must go beyond differences but not before differences with nothingness. We must go across differences and with the strength of differences. To have many differences is a good thing, not a bad thing. The conviction of the new genericity is not reducible to the pure nothingness of a class as in classical dialectics.

We must discover another manner of defining the affirmative dialectics which claims that genericity is different from nothingness. The affirmative potency of diversity can be included within genericity. At the ontological level we must affirm that genericity is not reducible to the immanent nothingness of being. This is why the generic is different from the universal, collective, and public. For the question of aesthetics, the point is that art searches for something like a generic form. It is a form which is not reducible to identity. For example, in the classical vision of painting, the form was something which had its identity through the imitation of nature. The point was that you had to find or invent a form which was an adequate representation of something existing in the world.

You must recognize the form across differences because there are different forms for different masters of painting. We recognize the form and so the form has an identity. But the movement of painting is to go beyond all of that. It is to go beyond the pure identity of the form and to create a form which is not defined strictly by its natural identity. You know, there was a rupture with imitation within the field of art, and so on. There was a movement toward a form that was not strictly dependent upon its natural or external identity. There was a movement toward a form which was not exactly a representation but which was nonetheless something like a representation. The form was a representation but it was also something else. There is a movement in the direction of the emancipation of the form which is also a movement in the direction of the genericity of the form. It is a movement toward a form that is not a coherent global form for the work of art and that is not submitted to identity. Often we can not recognize something without a proper identity. But we have forms which are generic in nature and which are the composition of formal differences in the painting. In the work of art, as in other truth procedures, the goal is to find something generic. We find the same sort of thing in the field of forms and we call it a new genericity.

There is a difficult relationship between the genericity of forms and the public. For example, in politics, it is difficult for an ordinary public to recognize the genericity of forms without any support from identity. This is why the movement of painting is also the movement of successive, scandalous, inventions. It is a movement against the common opinion. There is an obscure passion, a passion of the inside, which is against genericity. Fascism, nationalism, but also academicism [laughter]; and against science, we have obscurantism. Obscurantism, academicism, fascism, and nationalism hate genericity and love identity. It is striking that this is true in the field of artistic creation and not only within the field of politics. There have been violent circumstances related to all of this in the artistic field: the first of the Sacred Spring of Stravinsky, riots against the paintings of Monet, and riots against new works of art. There is a passion for identity and a hatred of genericity. It is a big part of ideological history and it holds in all fields.

The second question was not completely clear for me, but it related to the status of aesthetics. There was a question relating to the distinction between aesthetics and the concrete process of the work of art because aesthetics is an ambiguous word. Aesthetics is something like a general name for every sort of knowledge of art, every explanation of art, and all philosophies of art, but aesthetics has an ambiguous relationship to artistic creation as such. I think that aesthetics can be objective and/or normative. We can name aesthetics that which is descriptive and historical and relates to the history of artistic creation and the history of forms, with detailed descriptions of these sorts of things, and so on. But aesthetics is very often normative insofar as it makes claims about good art and the norms for artistic creation. It is a form of judgment.

In any case, aesthetics is a secondary operation because it is the supposition of the existence of works of art. Aesthetics is the name of the relationship between philosophy, art, and history. And so it is not a creation of truth because it is the work of art itself which is the creation of truth. The work of art is the creation of genericity in forms whereas aesthetics is reflexive and comes after the creation of forms. The goal of aesthetics is not artistic, it is philosophical. You know, philosophy always comes after the work of art, after scientific invention, and so on. Hegel claimed that philosophy came at the end of the day, at the beginning of the night. I accept that philosophy comes after, it is true. We are the avant-garde before, and philosophers after.

The other question asked about the possibility of a change in the visual arts that is not linked to a change of technology. There is certainly a relationship between art and technology. For example, we can point to the creation of cinema as a technological advancement in the field of art. But there have also been great artistic movements without a strong relationship to technological change. For example, the invention of theater and tragedy in Greece, and the history of painting is certainly in a relationship with some aspects of geometry but not of technology. Two of the great European revolutions in the field of music were the invention of tonality and the invention of serialism, the first was in the 16th century and the second was in the beginning of the last century. Neither of these had a relationship to technology. Poetry has practically nothing to do with technology, and so on. I think that it is a false idea to claim that the development of art is closely linked to the development of technology. It is not true.

Certainly, we can argue in the reverse that some technological inventions can be appropriated by artistic creation. But it is not a necessity nor is it a pure causality. I think that it is dangerous to exaggerate the function of technology in all of the fields of human existence. Technology is certainly spectacular, but it also moves with the rhythm of transformation within the capitalist world. Technological change is the fundamental type of change within the capitalist world. Technological change is linked to the capitalist world because of the possibility that exists for opening up new markets and offering new products. Capitalism necessitates the offering of new products, or of products of a different nature, and this is the constant change of the big market. In some sense, the ideology of decisive importance for capitalist ideology is related to technological change. I'm convinced of this point.

We must be cautious about the question of technology. When there exists a relationship between artistic creation and technology, it is very often also a critique of technology and not necessarily an appropriation of technology. There are fundamental critiques made through the work of art about the form of superficial change that comes with technological progress. There are also philosophical criticisms of technology, and so on. In my opinion, the true position is to discover what we can do outside of the ideology of technological change. We must preserve the possibility for a change which has no relationship to technological transformations. In some sense, this is a neutral position because it does not exaggerate our technological destiny. It does not claim at the beginning that technology brings real change and that without technology we have nothing at all because we live in the modern technological world, and so on. It also does not claim that technology is evil and is responsible for the devastation of the planet and the end of humanity. These two positions are symmetrical, and they are false positions. They are both inside of the world of technology. It is much more interesting to claim that technology exists but that it is not so important.

The last question concerned architecture and its difference from other forms of art. It is a very interesting because architecture is by necessity a part of the inside. In this respect, the relationship between architecture and power is of historical importance. Practically all of the big monuments have been religious monuments, imperial monuments, monarchic monuments, or, finally, republican monuments. Modern architecture has been a form of power in of itself, but it is an economic power and not a political power. Architecture, even as a private form of creation, is within the hands of financial potency. If architecture strives to create something from the outside it is usually as a compromise with the inside. Contemporary architecture is largely a compromise because the process of creation costs too much money, and where there exists too much money there always also exists a compromise.

This is what is so interesting about architecture. What are the new compromises? What is the process of the invention of the possibility of new compromises? What forms of architecture are accepted by the state and by power and what forms come from outside and are therefore not a pure monument of power? The creation of a new central piece of architecture in a big town always involves a big discussion but usually the discussion happens among those concerned with private property rather than among those interested in new forms of power. Under capitalism, private property affirms, or is on the side of, novelty because this is one of its methods of propaganda. You know, it is very difficult for a big capitalist to say: "Oh, I am absolutely against novelty!" The capitalist embraces an ideology of change and so he also embraces an ideology of novelty. The paradoxical result is that, in the field of architecture, we can find some forms of invention which are on the side of private property. For example, a bank with their private houses made by inventive architects.

Next, we have a question concerning life and death.

Student: I would like you to expand on the notion of death within the framework of change that we've been working through. I have two questions: if death is only for the other, because the person or the thing that dies doesn't know, is it an event? And, if there could be something such as death as such, if we could name it like that, would it be the negation or absence of change?

Badiou: This question concerns death and the dialectics of life and death. We have here the opening of a discussion which is actually a very interesting and complex one. First, there is the very old idea that we have no knowledge of death but only an idea of the death of others. And so we have no experience of death. The question of death must be examined from the point of view of my death and of the death of others. It is a question of the death of others and of our own proper death. We do not know our own proper death, we can only have knowledge of the death of others.

This position is absolutely inside of the empiricist vision of knowledge. Effectively, we have no knowledge of our proper death and we can have no experience of the proper death of others. To provide an example of the problem: you are white and you have no internal experience of what it is to be black. The conclusion is that we have no knowledge of what it is to be black. No, I claim that knowledge can in fact be transmitted, and it can in fact be universalized. For example, there are works of art – novels, movies, and so on – that clearly explain and transmit what it is to be black. We can also transmit the death of the other. The process of death exists and the death of the other is also a perfect knowledge of death itself. Certainly, it is not at the level of personal experience, but that is not my question. My question is: what is the death of a historical point of view? What is the relationship of the collective to death as such?

We can not claim that death is nothing because death exists. It is not because I can not understand my proper death that death has a social existence. I know what my terrible suffering is when somebody else is dead, and so on. It is the same thing for many experiences which are not personal and intimate but are experienced as the negation of others. It is why I do not completely agree with this point; not only for the question of death but also for the question of the possibility to have a personal experience of what being is. I think that subjective transmission exists. A subjectivity can be transmitted. But it is not because we have knowledge from others that this knowledge becomes purely objective. You can have a subjectivation of the experience of others. When somebody communicates his proper experience to us we experience an affect, and so we can not claim that only true personal experience is intimate and reflexive.

Death is absolutely present at the level of the collective and at the level of personal consciousness. The attempt to reduce death to nothing except for the religious promise of something after death is an absolutely false attempt. The question is, what is the collective relationship to the existence of death? The existence of death is not absolutely something biological, medical, and so on, it is a subjective question. It is not only found with the fear of death but also in the fact that death is absolutely present in our collective existence. I insist on this point because I think that the attempt to reduce the question of death to nothing or to a religious question renders death uninteresting except for the populations in capitalism who treat death as personal.

In fact, the moment of death as a moment of the subject is not interesting for everybody. It is not a consumer question. An old man can be interesting to a population for many reasons. Sometimes an old man has money. We can organize some really different practices for old men and women, but after his death, after we burn his corpse, it is nothing. But it is false that it is nothing. It is absolutely false. We must collectively recognize the mortality of an old man, and this is why it is important for us to invent a new symbolism of death which is not of a religious nature. If we can not invent a new symbolism concerning death, one that is not religious, then we prepare for the return of religion. For a long time it has been acceptable that to die is nothing. Death is a situation that a man or a woman encounter at the end of their life and the collective must invent something which recognizes the fact that there is death and that there is suffering.

There is a very important question concerning time in relation to death. It relates to the constitution of memory, the existence of memory, and so on. Religion answers these questions. I am not a religious man, but I can understand that. The possibility of the death of god, in Nietzschean language, is also the possibility that we can not say anything about death. And so today everybody dies alone. Alone, because there is no collective recognition. There is no general and symbolic recognition concerning the place of this man and this woman in our world. In the old times, the church was here to answer this question. Today, power is not here, it is absent. It is a remarkable fact. There is no presentation of collective power when somebody dies. The argument was that the church once answered this question, but today it is impossible for something to come after the church and to be here in the name of a collective when somebody dies.

This is a dangerous argument. We know that for a very long time prehistoric man had public ceremonies for the dead. After many years that possibility disappeared. And so I am not convinced by this argument. When I claim that we must find a non-religious answer to the question I do not mean to suggest that it is not okay for somebody who is religious to find a solution. It is a very important question and not at all something which can be reduced to the fact that death is nothing. If we restrict ourselves to the death of others then it is a question of biology and an objective question concerning the disintegration of the body. And if it is something else, then it is religious.

But I will return to your question. I maintain that we must discover a new dialectics of life and death. Death as such can not be an event because, at the level of the individual body, death is a closure of possibility. It is an interdiction of possibility and so, in some sense, death is a counter-event. What can we do with a counter-event? We must transform something which is purely a counter-event into something which is for the collective and has a positivity. Naturally, this was once the work of the church. The church claimed that there was a future after death. In any case, if we can not claim something like that then we can at least not remain mute because to be mute is to accept the savage law of the contemporary world.

I think that you know that the collective can be judged according to two fundamental points. First, it can be judged according to its relationship to old people, and second, it can be judged according to its relationship with death. These are not the same things. And so these are two fundamental points concerning what I name civilization. I think the collective is a civilization when it does have some collective symbolization concerning death. This is the point of civilization. A collective is a civilization when all people are productive and not only destructive to the collective. Productive, because, what can we do concerning the negative part of life, concerning the aged?

We must return to the question of tradition. Traditionally, we have had two answers to these two questions. The old man and the old woman have been in charge of the transmission of tradition and their death has been the passage to something else. We must organize the civilization for this passage. Okay, we can not claim that the old man and the old woman must transmit the repetition of tradition, and we can not affirm that there is a future after death. But we must say something. If we accept nothing then it is the defeat of civilization. This is important also in relation to the radical critiques of capitalism. Capitalism is not only the question of social inequalities and financial crises. Capitalism is also an anthropology, it is also a vision for old men and old women. And progressively, many aspects of civilization have disappeared. In fact, this is why capitalism is contemporaneous with the death of god. It is an adequate world for the death of god because it harbors a purely terrestrial definition of happiness without any promise.

I think capitalism is the consequence of the death of god and not the solution of the problem opened up by the death of god. These are not the same things. Capitalism is within the problem of the death of god and is within the desperation of symbolizing death as a passage. Capitalism is not the solution to the problem. It is not the solution to the problem of the death of god for humanity, it is only a pure consequence. The life of capitalism is installed within the situation of the death of god but it is not at all an answer to the general question of the death of god. The desperation of heroism is also in some sense a consequence of the death of god because god was the parent of ideas in the old world. There is a difficulty of obtaining a general and global conviction as a consequence of the death of god. And so we do not have the possibility for heroism. The question of civilization and death, the question of the function of the old man and woman, and finally the question of the destiny of truth in general, are really the questions of our world. Because these are questions concerning the world without god.

I can accept that god is dead. I can accept it. He is dead. But I can not accept that the ordinary world that we live in today is a solution to the problem opened up by the death of god. But there are many concrete questions left for us. What is the real positive function of old people in society? What is the destiny of truths? Why is there a desperation involved for heroism? It is a part of our overall discussion. So we will stop here.

[applause]

Day Five

Seminar Eight

*Regular change & singular change * Multiplicities, objects, localizations, orders, and worlds * There is no world of the worlds * Reflexivity, transitivity, anti-symmetry * The maximum & minimum * Wittgenstein and the limits of a world * It is much easier to be one than to exist * The picture inside the world * Being & existence*

Good afternoon. I propose that we begin today with explanation of the concept of world and the general theory of regular change. The most important distinction is between regular change and singular change. The main point is that regular change is a change which is completely inside the laws of the world, and singular change, or an event, is something like an immanent exception inside of the world. In the second session we will discuss the last three questions. And tomorrow we will finish studying the question of singular change in relation to regular change if we do not do so today. So we will discuss an event as a specific form of singular change. After all of that we will turn to the reading and interpretation of a poem by [Paul] Valéry.

I recall that the question of the world is very important because a change is always a change in a particular world. We can not speak of a world and of a change in general because the world is a localization of multiplicities. There is not only being as such but also being somewhere. In German, this is *dasein,* or to be here. The world is the thinking of *dasein.* We can claim that the world is a topological concept insofar as it is a concept which is related to the question of localization. At the very abstract level we can only claim that a world is a place where multiplicities of multiplicities become objects, they become objects of the world. It is only a change of name for them. In other words, multiplicities are sets, and when they are localized in a world we can name them the objects of the world. And so localization is also objectivation, localization is objectivation. It is the passage from pure being to being here or being there, and that is the form which an object takes.

The point is that to understand localization is also immediately to understand the question of order. But, order of what? Precisely, order of differences, order between different places in the world, and order from the evaluation of the intensity of existence in a world. Recall that at the level of pure being the question of intensity does not exist. Being is a pure multiplicity and so it is something extensional. It is not the same thing in a world, where the multiplicity takes the order of an intensity. We also know that there are differences between different identities. The identity between two multiplicities in a world can be different from another difference of identity between two multiplicities in a world. You see, when a multiplicity is in a world there is immediately a sort of multiplicity of relations with other multiplicities which are different measures. Sometimes the difference can be with the same intensity.

So, when a multiplicity is in a world there are also, immediately, a great number of relations as well. In fact, localization is a system of relations between a multiplicity and other multiplicities of the same world. If you want, it is a sort of geography of multiplicities and not only of affirmations of the multiplicities or of the being of multiplicities. This point is very important because a change of that sort of system of relations defines the being there of the multiplicity. The multiplicity has not only *sein* but also *dasein,* has not only being but also being there, and it is defined by the system of relations between the multiplicity and another multiplicity of the same world.

We must examine the difference between all of these relations. There is not only one relation, but there are many relations between all objects of a world. An order is a possibility to claim that one multiplicity is more or less identical to another which is also more of less different from another, and so on. There are many examples of something like that. Naturally, somebody can be in a social world. If a person is in a social order then this means that there are different types of relations with other persons that exist in that social order or world. All of these relations can be examined from the point of view of the order. For example, you can have a closed relationship to your parents and you can have a closed relationship to many other person in strange countries, and so on. The simple example of an order consists of the measure of relationships between one multiplicity and another multiplicity within the same world and not the relationship inside of being itself. For example, a human being might be different from another human being in the geographical sense, insofar as each human being lives in a different country. And so for those human beings that live in a strange country, you do not know them. You can say that they are indifferent to your existence. There is practically no relation between you and them. And so it is a relation with a minimal degree of existence, with something like zero existence, or with a near zero existence.

This explains why we can have nationalism, racism, and so on. Nationalists always claim something like: "they are not absolutely in the same world as mine; my world is first of all my country and my race." A world is always something like that. A world is a system of relations and so it is also a system of proximity, or a degree of the measure of the proximity of change within the same world. There is an example of this in the declaration made by the French fascist [Jean-Marie] Le Pen. He is the chief of the Front Nationalist, a political organization in France. To repeat him: it is absolutely natural to first of all prefer myself to others, second of all to prefer my family to others, and third, to prefer French people to strangers. After that, we can prefer some strangers to others, and so on. This is typically fascist reason because it reduces the world to the part of the world with strong relationships.

In fact, this is a topological point of view. The position states that what is good is near to me. Alas, it is a very common idea. We see that the world is linked to the idea of order. We can say that the abstract definition of a world is first of all the multiplicity of multiplicities, or, the objects of the world, and second of all it is a measure concerning the relations. So the most simple form is something like the following:

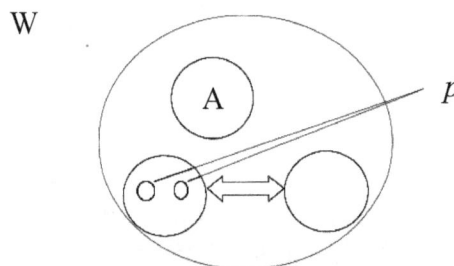

You have the world, which has within it a system of multiplicities, and you have an order. In fact, the order remains within the world, and so we name the world an order. The order is a structure. We can say something else concerning this structure, but there is a structure. The order provides a measure for two elements of an object, which is *p*. After that, it is much more complex. There is the possibility for a confrontation between the relation and another relation between from the multiplicities [the double sided arrow]. For our philosophical understanding today we are not obliged to go into all of the technical details. This technical discussion is explicitly developed in my book *Logics of Worlds.*

You see, the abstract discussion of a world is a very simple one. We have the multiplicity of multiplicity and the possibility to evaluate the identity or difference between two elements of a multiplicity inside of a world. And we have *p* as an element of the structure of order. So we can begin with a very simple idea: a world is a multiplicity of multiplicities with a sort of immanent possibility to create a relationship inside of a world, which is something like an order, or something like an evaluation of an order. The simplest concept of the world is a collection of multiplicities with an order, and the particularity of the world is rather the particularity of the order of the order, or of the structure of the order. It is why the same multiplicity can be localized in different worlds. This point is of absolute necessity for our discussion. It is not the presence of a particular multiplicity which is a definition of the world. The definition of the world is the effect on multiplicity by the structure of the world itself. This is what I name the localization of the multiplicity, inside of a world.

Nothing is opposed to the idea that the same multiplicity can be exposed in different worlds. When the multiplicity is exposed in different worlds, they can have different relations to other multiplicities. It is an empirical experience. In our concrete existence, we are often in different worlds. We change in time, and the world is not the same for us. More precisely, if the world is an order that defines relations then our experience is very often to pass from a world into another world. Even my relation to another human being can be different in different contexts. It is a common experience. I can have some form of a relationship with a friend in the context of my job and maybe it is a completely different relationship in the more private context. This has been crucial for the work of the novel, because the novel is the art of exposing the change of the world. The novel attempts to demonstrate how the same subject can be different from different points of view. These different points of view are different contexts and so they are also different worlds, in some sense.

A world is not at all what we today name the universe. A universe is a totality. For the concept of world as I propose it here, there is no possibility for totality properly speaking. There is a context, there are some multiplicities, and there is an order, but we can also have other contexts and other worlds. It is possible to prove that a totality does not exist. There is no world of the worlds. There is no total world. It is possible to demonstrate that the total universe or the world of worlds is a contradictory concept. [Bertrand] Russell demonstrated this at the beginning of the last century. Concretely, the proof demonstrates that the set of all sets is contradictory. It is a mathematical proof. We can not assume the existence of the set of all sets without assuming a logical contradiction, and so the idea of totality is also a contradictory idea. *The* world can not exist.

In some sense, a world is also a multiplicity. There exists a plurality of worlds. Finally, a world is defined by some multiplicities but also by an order. But there exists many different sorts of orders. That is the point. Different structures of order are possible. With the same multiplicities, we can have many worlds; with the same objects, we can have many worlds. Before being elaborated by philosophy or science, I think that this idea was evident for artistic creation. For artistic creation, variations are obtained using practically the same elements. Maybe these are not exactly the same elements, but they are practically the same elements. This is striking for painting. For example, if you look at the history of painting in the Netherlands within twenty years, you will notice that there are many elements in common in the image, structure, and representation of the painting. Many elements are absolutely identical and so we can claim that it is the same world, except that, artistically speaking, it is not the same world because some paintings are universal and some paintings are only repetitions. Today, it is important to expose not only paintings that are beautiful but also paintings that are not so beautiful. It is very interesting to see the difference. It is not a true difference, but it is, precisely, a difference of artistic worlds. Some paintings are good precisely because they repeat, they present the common elements of the painting of the time. And some paintings are very different, they have the same elements but they have a different localization; a difference of light, a difference of just one important detail, and so on.

We can experience the possibility of having a different world using the same elements, but with a difference or change of the relationship between these elements. It is a change of the order. It was, first of all, a very old artistic experience. If you observe the Roman sculptures there is also a very important repetition. Sometimes you can see the face of the man but sometimes there is something different, with the same elements but with a change of the details. It is with a change of the relationship between all of the elements that we find something absolutely new. The artistic experience is the experience of the possibility of composing worlds that have the same elements but are nonetheless different worlds.

Maybe this is even more striking in the field of novels. If you read novels from the nineteenth century you will notice that they are very often similar. They very often have the same elements. And so it is the same multiplicity, the same story, the same persons. But there also exists some elements that are more important than others, not because they are outside of the multiplicity of elements but because the world with these elements is different. We can speak of the world of a great novel because the order or the structure of the novel is different. So, a world is a collection of multiplicities with an order. An order is fundamentally a dissymmetrical relation with two terms. Which is, generally, something like this. Can everybody can see?

$$p \leq q$$

For example, we have something like that. You can read it as follows: *p is smaller or equal to q.* You know, there is a dissymmetry here which must be examined. The negative affirmation is contained in the statement that *if p is smaller than q, then it is impossible that q will be smaller than p.* This is why, really, it is a dissymmetrical relation. Three properties are important for the general context of thinking.

First, reflexivity:

$$p \leq p$$

Reflexivity can be written as follows: *p is smaller than or equal to p.* Why? It is because we have equal in the definition, it is smaller *or equal*. And so the relationship is dissymmetrical in general, but it is symmetrical for the same term. The term is linked to itself by the relation of order. It is why we can claim that it is a reflexive relation.

Second, transitivity:

$$p \leq q \;\&\; q \leq t$$
$$p \leq t$$

Transitivity can be written as follows: *if p is smaller or equal to q, and q is smaller or equal to t, then p is smaller or equal to t.* Why is this called transitivity? It is because the relation transmits first from *p* and *q* onto *q* and *t*, and then also transmits or conserves the relation from *p* to *t*. The general logic of transitivity is of some importance for many fields of thinking. For example, a father's son can also be the father of somebody, but the son of this son is also from the same family. It is a transitive relationship.

The third property is anti-symmetry:

$$p \leq q \;\&\; q \leq p$$
$$p = q$$

If p is smaller or equal to q, and q is smaller or equal to p, then this signifies that p is equal to q. Okay? If the relation is symmetrical – *p is smaller or equal to q and q is smaller or equal to p* – then the fact is that we do not have two different terms. They are equal. Only two equal terms can define the symmetry of the relationship. If the two terms are different then the relationship is dissymmetrical. One is smaller than the other but the other can not be smaller than the first. Naturally, we accept that these are equal.

An order is a very simple structure. Moreover, I insist on the point that it is a fundamental structure. It is the basis for many scientific operations, it is the basis for something very fundamental in all forms of mathematics. And it is a basic conceptual construction of thinking about a world. So, I will repeat: an order is a relation between a set of terms. It is the relation between some elements of a set, with three properties: reflexivity, transitivity, and anti-symmetry. When we have an order we also have a possibility for a comparison between the terms. In fact, we can claim that an order is the abstract form of possible comparisons between two terms. It is why we claim that the first is smaller than the other or that the first is inferior with respect to the other.

All of that relates to the interpretation of the abstract structure itself. You see, in the case of the world, the order organizes the comparison between identities. This is perhaps the central question. If we have an order, then with this order we can organize the comparison between identities. In fact, the order of a world has some other properties, and not just the strict properties heretofore discussed. For concrete reasons I can not go into all of the details, but one property is of interest. An order has a maximum and a minimum:

$$p \leq M \ \& \ \mu \leq p$$

We have the maximum [M] and minimum [μ]. Now, what is a maximum and what is a minimum? It is very simple. The maximum is a term which is bigger than all other terms. Or, we can claim that the maximum is smaller than no terms, because it is bigger than all other terms. If you take the term p: *p is smaller or equal to M.* It is impossible to have the reverse claim. The minimum is a term which is smaller than all other terms. If you have a term p: *μ is smaller or equal to p.* Why, philosophically speaking, …

[interruption: Badiou's teaching assistant brings over another whiteboard]

Thank you, thank you. This is a good point of organization, in our world [laughter]. What is the existence of a maximum and minimum in the context of an order of the world? Wittgenstein named this the question of the limits of the world. Maybe the world is infinite, but even if the world is infinite there are limits inside of the world. What sort of limits? Limits of possible intensity. A world can not admit an intensity which is without any limit. The world is a potency of localization but it is also a potency of limitation with respect to the intensity of existence in the world. Maybe the world can not accept that it would be too hot. That is a limit. It is a concrete example. More generally, for a world there always exists a limit inside of the order and this limit does not concern the number of objects. The number of objects can be infinite, there can be an infinity of objects.

It is very interesting for us that Wittgenstein, in his *Tractatus,* wrote a very striking sentence: the limits of my language means the limits of my world. The limits of my language are also the limits of the world. You know, this means that there is something which can not be said. But if something can not be said then it is also, in some sense, that this something which can not be said is something which is not in the world. Maybe it is in another world. In the complete theory of the order of the world, we can have a proof that if a maximum exists then there also exists a minimum. It is a very simple proof, so I will not give it to you [laughter]. Philosophically, the idea of maximality and minimality in a world brings us to the field of change. For example, the question of the language inside of the question of change: how can I change the language to name something which I could not name before? It is the question of invention within language.

It is the question of poetry. Perhaps poetry is the creation of the possibility of saying something which could not be said through the ordinary means of language. This is probably a good definition of poetry: the attempt to name, or the attempt to inscribe, in language something which could not be said within the ordinary limits of language. And so the ordinary limits of language are also the ordinary limits of what could be said within the concrete world that we know. This is why Wittgenstein affirmed that the limits of language are also the limits of the world. We always have a limit within the circumstances of what can be said. To say something more, perhaps we must pass into another world. This is why it is common to claim that the world of poetry is not exactly the common world. Maybe it is the truth of the common world, but it is not the common world.

Here, we are within the theory of the common world. The change of the world is another problem. We admit that there is a limit. And if there is a maximum, then it is unique. There is only one maximal term possible. This will be my only proof during my seminar today. Suppose we have two maximal terms [M & M']. If these terms are maximal, we have by necessity the following:

$$Terms:\ M,\ M'$$

$$M \leq M'$$

$$M' \leq M$$

$$M = M'$$

A maximum is bigger or equal to all terms, and so it is also bigger or equal to another maximum. But the other maximum is also a maximum. So we have $M = M'$. But, by the axiom of anti-symmetry, if we have $M \leq M'$ and $M' \leq M$, then you have $M = M'$. Finally, we can not have two different maximums. It is a small exercise [laughter].

It is very interesting because it is the first time that we have had a property which is, by itself, a property of a term which is unique. In fact, this is the classical demonstration of the universality of god. What is god? God is a maximum term. It is not possible to have two gods because one is superior to the other, and the other is superior to the first. So they are equal. It is certainly difficult to find a real proof for the existence of god, but the proof of the fact that there is only one god is possible [laughter]. It is much easier to be one than to exist [laughter]. It is a very complex property. And it is why the mystic vision is that god is one. The mystic conviction is that the unicity of god is in some sense the very existence of god. There is a fusion between existence and unicity. Rationally, we can prove that there is only one god. It is very difficult to prove that god exists, but the mystical perception of the existence of divinity is that the relationship is one. The unicity is itself a proof of existence but it is not a mathematical proof. It is a proof by the pure feeling of the mystical subject. This is why there is always a conflict between the mystical vision of god and the rational vision of god.

To return to the question of order, we can have interesting properties from the maximum and minimum:

$$id(x,y) = p \qquad \{ p \leq q$$
$$id(x,z) = q \qquad \{ p < q$$

First: *the identity of these two elements [x and y] are equal to p.* With the order of the measure of identity of the two elements, we could have also: *the identity of x with another term, q.* And we can compare their identities. That is the point. For example, *if p is effectively smaller than q, and if p is not equal to q, then we can say that the identity of x to this one [y] is radically less than the identity of x to this one [z].* Okay?

$$id(x,y) < id(x,z)$$

This is of fundamental importance for the world. We have the concrete means to have a comparison between the different identities of the terms. So we can take one term [*X*], which is in a relationship with many other terms:

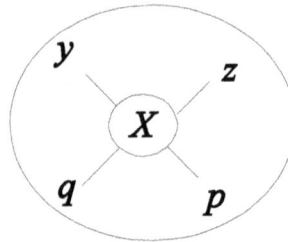

If you have a term inside of a world with many other terms then you have a relation of identity between all of the terms. We can have a comparison of all of these identities. Finally, we can have something like a picture of the term inside of the world. We can define the terms by the complete system of identities between them. For example, there a the complete system of relations in a great novel, a complete system of relationships between one person in the novel and other persons in the novel. Progressively, there are descriptions of the relations between different identities of the person in relation to others and different identities of others in relation to the person. Progressively, there is a sort of picture of the being, the multiplicity, within the world of the novel. When we have a world, and an order of the world, we also have the possibility to describe the presence of a term within the world. The presence of a term in the world is a system of identities and differences with all of the other different terms.

If we have a measure of identity, then we must also have a measure of difference. For example:

$$id(x,y) = p$$
$$id(x,z) = q$$

$$p < q$$

If we have the identity of *x* and *y*, and we have the identity of *x* and *z*, then we have *p* as absolutely different from *q*. We can claim that the difference between *x* and this term [*y*] is much more important than the difference between this term [*x*] and this term [*z*]. The identity between this one and this one [*x* and *y*] is less than the identity between this one and this one [*x* and *z*].

Naturally, when the identity is less, the difference is more. We can not only have a comparison of identities but we can also have an identification or comparison of differences.

We have the maximum and minimum as the limits of differences. If, for example, we have something like this:

$$id(x,y) = M$$

If the identity of x and y is a maximum [M], then we can claim that x and y are, in a world, practically the same. It is not possible to be more identical to x than to M. On this point, there is something important, but the intuition of it is very difficult. If the identity between x and y is maximal then we can claim that x and y are the same terms in a world. You know, maybe as human beings they are completely different, because the maximal identity is only a specific evaluation of identity and difference in a world and relative to the order of a world. Perhaps x and y are not completely identical in other circumstances, in another world or another order. In another world where the maximum is different, x and y can also be different. It is not an empirical impossibility.

Two persons can have the same existence in a world. For example, we can take the capacity of being good at mathematics. Within a world, there is an order which specifies that somebody is better at mathematics than another, and so on. In this world, which is the world of learning, maybe there are two persons whom have the same strength in mathematics. They produce the same results, and they are identical. By a change of world, the sameness is not the same. The identity is different because there was a change in the measure of the identities. It is evident in our concrete experience, it is not at all an abstraction. We perfectly know that it is possible for us to be very good at something or appreciate in some world and for this not to be the case in another world or under different circumstances.

It is a question of order. What is the structure for comparison in the world? You know, a world is a localization and therefore it offers the possibility of comparison. This possibility of comparison can be different when we are not in the same world. So we have the possibility of the identity of two terms relative to the world, even if they are completely different ontologically. From the point of view of ontology, they are two different multiplicities. It is why we often have a relation of sameness between two things in a world which are ontologically different. This point is central.

You know, all of this comes down to the difference between being and existence. Existence is the being-there of a world, it is being in a world. It is a classical name. It is one of the possible translations of *dasein*. In French, for example, *dasein* has been translated as existence. But, precisely, *dasein* is different from *sein*. Being is different from being-there. At the level of being some things can be different, and at the level of a world, the same things can be the same. Refer again to your own experience. In some world, the relationship you have with somebody is completely qualitative and in some other circumstances the relationship to the same person is different. You have concrete examples.

A world is not an empirical totality of everything that exists. The world is always relative to the structure of order immanent to the world. We can perfectly explain why there are many experiences of identity by accepting the claim that we live in many worlds. My claim is that the particularity of human beings, from among other animals, is marked by the possibility to live in an infinity of worlds. It is the possibility to displace existence within many worlds. When we are in the domain of living beings whom have simpler ways of life, there is the necessity for them to be in a fewer number of worlds. Some very simple animals can only be in a very defined world. They can not go outside, they live within very precise circumstances. And adapting life to many circumstances is more important as we go in the direction of the top of animal existence, which is the world of man-kind, our world. This is a possible definition of the place of animals in the hierarchy of life. Certainly, our form of being animals – human animals – is the capacity to adapt ourselves to life in many different worlds. And maybe it is also the capacity to be a subject and to accept an event. An event is a radical change of worlds for humanity because it is the possibility to accept a world which is very often a contradiction of the current world. It is the acceptance of a completely different world. It is really the possibility of creation, because it is the acceptance of something absolutely new, absolutely different from our world.

You see, we have the difference between *to be* and *to exist*. At the level of *to be* we can affirm that there is something invariant, that there is something which *is*. At the level of being in a world, we must affirm that there are many possibilities and many differences. In fact, all of that must be applied to the identity of the multiple to itself:

$$\frac{id(x,x) = p}{W}$$

The identity of x to x also has a measure in a concrete world [W]. The identity of x to x is the existence of x. And we can say that the existence of x is p. All of that is relative to the world [W]. It is not an absolute determination. There is no absolute determination of existence because existence is relative to a world with determination. As I have said, we also have the experience of being in some world and being in another world. It is a common experience. It is also the experience of a change of world. It is simple. To be timid is precisely to be afraid of changing the world. It is a fear of the change of world, it is a fear of having a true existence in another world.

Okay, so we can translate all of that into the concrete vision of our existence. The point is that we can examine two interesting possibilities in the world. The possibilities are:

$$Ex=M \ (in \ W)$$

$$Ex=\mu \ (in \ W) \text{ - } in\text{-}existent$$

The existence of x is equal to the maximum [M] in a world; the existence of x is equal to a minimum [μ] in a world [W]. If an existence is maximal then we can claim that the term x is absolutely in the world. It can not be in the world more than it already is. It is the situation in which the term x is completely appropriated by the world. It is when we have the conviction that

82

the world is very good. It is when we can claim that it is perfect, it is a very good world. In the world of morality, it is when we have the feeling of doing what we must do, and so on.

All of that is the feeling of the maximality of the relationship to yourself in a world. It is the maximality of your proper identity in the world. Naturally, in a world where the existence is minimal we have the idea of being practically outside of the world. You are not really inside. It is what it means to be a stranger to the world, a stranger in the night. The technical or philosophical way to explain this is to claim that you are an in-existent of the world. Because, in some sense, you do not exist in the world. You are in the world because your being is there, but you do not exist. This is the most important difference between being and existence. You may not exist, you might be, but you may not exist. It is a possibility.

We can have a proof that there is some form of unicity of the in-existents. We can prove that two in-existents are the same, in some sense. It depends on some properties of the order. There is a very singular place of in-existence in a world and maybe it is also the place of suffering or negativity. You know that you are in a world and you know that you in-exist in this world, that you are nothing, and that nothing is not ontological because you are still something ontologically. But in the world, you are nothing. And so to be nothing in the world is simply to claim that your existence is minimal. For the world, to be minimum is to be zero. It is like you are not in the world, but you are in the world. In existence, it is also common that you are somewhere but nobody recognizes that you are somewhere. Nobody gives any signification to your presence, nobody knows you, and so on. And so, you are nothing. You are in the experience of not being in the world in which you are.

It was exactly this position that Marx discussed. It was the place of the proletariat in the political world of the nineteenth century. I will give you an example. Naturally, the proletariat is a collective existence in the historical world of the society of the nineteenth century. But from the point of view of political domination, the proletariat did not exist. Domination was reserved for the bourgeois class. An event, a political event, a revolution, can be defined by the transformation of *no existence* into *real existence* in a world. In a word, a political revolution has the capacity to allow us to go from something minimal to something maximal:

$$Ex=\mu \rightarrow Ex=M$$

That is the abstract description of revolution [laughter]. Naturally, you understand, it is a change of worlds. It is properly speaking a change of worlds. If the evaluation of your existence is maximal and, before, the evaluation of your existence was minimal, then there are different orders. It is not the same order. So it is true that revolution, when defined like this, is really a change of worlds. It is the creation of another world. We will stop here today.

[applause]

Seminar Nine
*The unsayable & event * Regular change * Trace * The subject of love * Dialectics of life &*
*death * Knowledge and experience of death * Qualified life and the acceptance of suffering **
The religious question of death

Is everybody here? If somebody is not here then he is in-existent for our world. Only by an event can he gain some existence [laughter]. This student will read a question concerning some of the characteristics of an event. After that we will return to the question of death.

Student: In your opinion, is there an intrinsic connection between the unsayable and the event? Can there exist, within a poem, play, story or novel, an event or a moment of truth change that is only made possible by the silences and absences allowed for by language?

Badiou: So we have a question concerning the relationship between the event and the unsayable. In fact, this is a part of the question of an event. If there is something like an event then we must have something which is unsayable. In some sense, the unsayable is without any name. It is unnamed. Not only is it unsayable but it is also without any clear connection with existing language. And why? It is because what exists is always of a constructable nature in a common situation or an ordinary world. In the common world everything that exists can be named. This is why I also name the situation "the encyclopedic situation of the world" in *Being and Event.* If there is something new in the world, then it is a regular change.

You know that a regular change is a change inside of the world. How can we have a change inside of the world? I will explain that tomorrow. For now I will state that regular change is a form of change which is without any problems inside of a defined world. When something is new by the regular change then it is a sort of novelty with a name inside of the world. You can have a new invention without speaking of truth at all, you can have something new inside the world and with it you can have the possibility to name that sort of production with reference to the common language.

If there is something like an event then the event is outside of the common laws of the world. I will explain why tomorrow. But this is one of the possible definitions of an event: something which happens in the world without a clear correlation between this happening and the laws of the world. It is a rupture of the laws of the world. Generally speaking, there is no name for an event. There is no name within the common language. There is probably a sort of reciprocity or correlation between the event and the unsayable, as you have said.

You attempted to give an example from within the artistic field. But it is actually a general situation. It is a fact of language. It is the point where the language is not available inside of the world. More generally, there is no real name for an event. The question is, how can we observe the situation of that which happens without a name? The difficulty is that an event probably disappears. An event is not something which *is,* an event is something which *happens.* So there is a beginning for an event but there is also an end for an event. And perhaps the end is sometimes very near to the beginning. It is like a sudden light. The most striking example might be the love encounter. Just after the encounter you are seduced and you can not repeat the encounter. The initial encounter is lost. If you repeat the encounter, it is very artificial. Generally speaking, alas, it is impossible to repeat the encounter. If you do not do what was necessary from the encounter then you can not repeat the scene.

This is the general structure of an event. We can not clearly distinguish between the appearing and disappearing of an event. How can we have the consequences of an event if the event itself disappears? What are the consequences of a disappearance for the question of the vanishing causality of the event? It is a question of having a trace of the event. The event disappears but there is some trace of it within the world. What exactly is the trace? It is a difficult problem. In my first book, *Being & Event,* I have my first solution to the problem. In *Logics of Worlds,* I have my second solution. I have changed my mind concerning the answer to this question of the consequences of an event after the event has disappeared.

In *Being & Event* my position was that the trace of an event is something like the discovery of a name for the event. It is the possibility of inscribing the event by a name. A name can be any range of names, any syntactical signification; a name can be a place or a book. In any case, it is the inscription of an event. The difficulty was that we really have two events in one event. The first event is the appearing and disappearing of the event and the second is the invention of a name. It became very difficult because it thus means that we have something like two subjects. The first subject creates a name for the disappearing of the event and after that there is a subject who organizes the consequences of the event or the consequences of the name. And so my solution was an obscure one. It was obscure because it was like a double subjectivity through the creation of the consequences of the event: first it is the discovery of the name and second it was the constitution of the consequences of the event as the truth-procedure. A subject-for-the-name and a subject-for-truth. There is no rational reason that these are the same subjects because the invention of the name is a very particular operation, it is completely different from the organization of the consequences.

Naturally, there is a counter experience when you think of the love-event. The first name is something like "I love you". It is named something like this. Maybe it is the name of the lover him or herself. The subject who says "I love you" is not absolutely the subject of love because the subject of love is the relationship between the two. The true subject of love is at the level of the two and not at the level of the one. It is a subject who says "I love you" at the level of the one, but it happens that the one becomes two. So an event is this elementary situation. We must understand the difficulty: the subject who is naming the event can not be the same as the subject who is within the consequences of the event. If the subject who says "I love you" is exposed to failure then he has something like a false name. If it is not true that the other loves him or her, then it is a failure. Finally, we can have a false encounter, or something like that. It is clear that the subject of the invention of the name can not be the same as the subject of the consequences of the event. This was something which was unclear to me.

In *Logics of Worlds,* I proposed a more classical formulation: there is a trace of the event itself. The name exists as a trace of the event. We name the sayable of the event as a trace immanent to the event. It is the fact of the event but it is not the event itself because the event disappears. But there is a trace. It is not a subjective operation. It is an objective trace. This trace is the concrete beginning of the subject of the event. So, for an event there is something said which was unsayable. The trace is not inscribed in the common language. All events bring with them linguistic invention. To return to your example: when, in a poem or in a novel, there is the immanent experience of something which is not said inside the world, there is an attempt to produce something like an event.

Okay. That is my response to the first question. Another student has a question concerning life and death. It is a long question so please pay attention.

Student: In suggesting that the old men and women of the future will transmit a new tradition concerning the relations between life and death, change and tradition, and history and nature, you observe that "what is obscure, but also promising, in ecology is to invent a non-religious question of death." In general, you argue forcefully for the necessity of a new non-religious thinking of death in dialectical opposition to life. This is where I think I must disagree.

To begin with, I do not think that the concepts of death and life make an appropriate dialectical pairing. At the level of content, they are not sufficiently dialectical. That is, we can synthesize the data of biology, and so on, with the experience of *being* in order to say something about the content of life from two opposing positions; but the experience of *being* can tell us nothing about our own death with regard to its possibility for bringing together opposing modes of knowledge. Death is a half empty concept, allowing only an external objective description and not also an internal or phenomenological one. Our extrapolations from our own experiences of others dying can tell us nothing at all about the experience of dying as such. In short, life is a dialectical concept in itself, while death is not.

Moreover, in order to think about death dialectically – that is, from within and without, both subjectively and objectively – it is necessary to speculate about the experiential content of death as a concept. Such speculation is more or less religious by definition. Indeed, I mean to say that one can not invent a non-religious question of death because the questioning of death is the fundamental mode of religiosity. Perhaps we would not agree about this when I state it in this manner, so let me make the point another way. If Heidegger could characterize death as the impossibility of possibility and if Levinas could follow with a reversal of the formula of the possibility of impossibility, we can – accepting this movement of thought as one from the thinking of death as concrete nihilation of *dasein* to the thinking of death as the undefined space of the possibility of such nihilation – treat the word death as simply catachrestic, as always and necessarily reaching beyond itself. Either death is something that happens to others, in which case it is adequately enough described by biology, physics, and so on, or it is something that will happen to me, in which case it designates neither more nor less than radical uncertainty. Death offers no traces of experiences by which one might speculate about the content of death. Such speculation, then, is religious, that is; it is axiomatic without also being universally commonsensical.

Third, [...]

Badiou: Yeah, yeah [...]

Student: What remains, then, is a withdrawal from the very question of death as a concept, or rather a subtraction of that question from our field of thought. This withdrawal would take the form of a substantive dialectical opposition, one that itself withdraws dialectically from the life/death pairing and that is itself more properly dialectical. I would name this, somewhat hastily, the opposition of qualified life and suffering. I mean to say that this pairing would be what orients ecology at its best. Indeed, it orients all contemporary thinking that serves to invent a new relation between history and nature. I do not want to impose on your generosity and so I will forebear tracing out what I see to be the consequences of such a thinking, but I do want to say two things more. First, what makes this pairing a dialectical withdrawal from, or a dialectical reduction of, life and death, and second what makes each of these terms dialectical in itself.

The life/death pairing presses out beyond the boundaries of dialectical reason itself, necessarily becoming religious speculation when it takes up the question of death. To retreat a step, then, is to subtract death as a question. But to subtract death as a question is necessarily to subtract something from life. To subtract what? Life itself, life as itself, life *qua* life. What is life without life *qua* life, or what is life without its nature? It is life as history, qualified life. What then negates qualified life? What else but suffering? Suffering contains within itself the question of the relation of its objective character to its subjective character. It is a concept wholly determined by some dialectical interplay between nature and history, between what is happening to whom- or what-ever can count as one, can count as a sufferer; and what experience the one counted as sufferer has. So, we say the sea slug can not suffer. It has no central nervous system, no centre of experience. There is no *there* there, as Gertrude Stein once noted. Equally, suffering does not at all receive its adequate definition by some description that would be restricted to nervous systems and not just stimuli. It is equally and necessarily a felt reality, dialectically opposed to its ascriptive, objective reality, in any particular instance. Likewise, and in the same vein, qualified life, which can not in any instance be reduced to either the brute fact of living or to the liver's apprehension of being, concerns always the twin subjective-object in question; the value and viability of a life.

In sum, then, it seems to me that the question of ecology today must be that of the qualified life/ suffering pair. This dialectical withdrawal from life and death is at once both properly radical and radically continuous. It is committed to a particular tradition of questioning and to changing the law of change. I suggest this, having accepted as valid the rest of your argument as presented. Would you assent to the amendment?

Badiou: Thank you so much. Now, I will explain my answer now and then you will have the last word. I really disagree with you. It is not a mystery. I will clarify the points of my disagreement.

First, you claim that we can synthesize the content of life with that of our biological experience. You also claim that the experience of being tells us nothing about our own death. From the very beginning, all of this is not exactly true. To claim something about the content of life is not reducible to the possible synthesis of the data of biology. There is a difference in the concept of life at this level. When I speak of life, within the opposition of life and death, it is not at all in reference to a purely biological concept of life. From the very beginning, my concept of life is what we can also name a quality of life. And so the opposition between life and death is from the very beginning not only an opposition between what we can say biologically about life and what we can say objectively or subjectively concerning death. Both terms are of a historical nature.

Life is not life in its natural sense; rather, life in the sense of our natural and historical experience. I think we are on the same level – you and me – when, by life, we mean to say "historical life". It is the life of human beings, in all of its dimensions. These dimensions include the biological dimension of the body, but also the symbolic, historical, social, and political determination of existence.

From the very beginning, I do not completely understand why you reduce the possibility of thinking death to our personal experience of death. We spoke about this point yesterday. I can not exactly understand why you want to reduce the possible knowledge of death to the personal experience of death. After all, we know many things without any personal experience. Why should death be a pure experience? For example, we know perfectly that there are deaths of others. Why can the knowledge of the death of others not be considered a true knowledge of death? Why, by necessity, do you claim that only our proper experience of death is a true knowledge of death? I think that it would be terrible if we conceded a similar limitation in another field in relation to another term rather than death. There are many ways to communicate the experience of the death of the other and to think the experience of the death of the other. When you claim that death is something that happens to me, it is true, in some sense, but we know that, for me, death is also something which happens to somebody else. Whence death? Death can happen to somebody else. It happens to me because it happens to somebody else.

So there is an experience of death by the mediation of the death of the other, and it is a personal experience of death. But it is nonetheless an experience of the death of the other. This is a point concerning the possibility of the knowledge of death, and maybe it is also a point concerning the possibility of a sort of experience of death which is not a personal and immanent experience precisely because death is the end of the possibility of the experience itself. You claim that death is only an external, objective, description and not a phenomenological one. Certainly. But this is not an intrinsic limitation of knowledge by itself. There are many parts of knowledge that are not reducible to the knowledge of a phenomenological or intimate nature but are nonetheless true forms of knowledge. In some sense, the disagreement is epistemological. The question asks for the possible existence of a concept of death which is really something of our experience and knowledge in a true sense. It asks for this, even though we can not have an experience of the pure end of our experience. Naturally, it is a tautology.

After that, we also have a disagreement concerning dialectics. You claim that the thinking of death dialectically, that is, from within and without, both subjectively and objectively, is an example of dialectics. But the relation between the subjective and the objective is only an example of the dialectical process. It is not the intrinsic definition of dialectics. The dialectical process is the process of negativity or the process of contradiction. Certainly, the contradiction of subjectivity and objectivity is one of the contradictions, but there are many dialectical processes which do not concern the relationship between the subjective and the objective. For example, the dialectical process between history and nature might [not] be reduced to a form of dialectical process between subjectivity and objectivity because there is something objective in history and there is something subjective in nature. So I think that your definition of dialectics is too narrow.

I would like to return to your point: either death is something which happens to others, in which case it is adequately described by biology and physics, or it is something which happens to me, in which case it designates nothing. I think that this opposition is clearly false. Either death is something which happens to others, in which case it is adequately enough described by biology and physics. Not at all! Biology and physics are only the discussion of the objective part of death. The transmission of the subjective process of death, the experience of death, and so on, are not reducible to biology and physics. I believe that we know much more about death from literature and cinema than from biology and physics. On this point, too, there is something in your explanation of objectivity and subjectivity which is unclear for me.

We can have some transmission of the subjective relationship to death. My disagreement is at the level of epistemology but it is also at the level of dialectics in general, and in particular it is a disagreement about the possibility of knowing something about death. After all of that, I also disagree with your position regarding qualified life and suffering. I think that your definition of qualified life is perhaps incomplete. I agree with you, but qualified life signifies historical life. You call it the historical life, that is, the historical form of life and not the pure biological form of life. As I said, what you have named qualified life is what I have named life. It is a matter of precision.

And I can not understand why suffering is the name of the dialectical opposite of qualified life because, in my opinion, suffering is a possible part of qualified life. I do not understand why you isolate suffering, which is a part of any form of life and which is especially a part of historical life. I do not think that we can take this modality of experience as a term for a new dialectics without claiming that qualified life signifies something outside of suffering. So, the good life, in this sense, is the life which is not exposed to suffering. We have a dialectical relationship between qualified life and suffering. I think that this vision is really inside of our world. This is my strongest critique. I think it is inside of our world because the specific form of a qualified life is in fact the good life. The good life is in opposition to suffering.

For me, the example of qualified life is not at all reducible to an opposition of suffering. In fact, if we define a true qualified life as a life which is exposed to the possibility of the process of a truth, or a life which is in a relationship to an idea, then suffering can simply be a part of the process. If you reduce the question concerning to the opposition of life and death to an opposition between qualified life and suffering then you assume the position of the contemporary world. Today, we can explain that the dominant opinion is that we must have a qualified life, a historical life, without suffering. It is a dialectical vision which is specific to the our particular world. It is related to one of the questions asked yesterday about the vision of a world without any heroism. Heroism is precisely the acceptance of suffering within the vision of a qualified life.

Suffering can not be one of the dialectical polarities for the opposition between historical life and nature because suffering also has two sides. There is a type of suffering which is historical in nature and there is another type of suffering which is biological in nature. So, I can not understand why you choose suffering as one of the terms for the new dialectics between historicity and nature. Literally, I can not understand this sentence: "what negates the qualified life? What else but suffering?" I can not understand this question! [laughter] I think that suffering can only be a negation of qualified life through a very weak conception of qualified life.

I can stop here. But, just to give you a sense of all of this: I think that my disagreement is first of all epistemological because I claim that you are brutally and absolutely an empiricist concerning death. That is, there is no truth of something if we do not have personal and sensible experience of it. As a historical proof, I think that it this is not true for death. After that, we have a disagreement concerning the world in which we are claiming that it is acceptable to have a vision from the position of suffering. I claim that suffering is a question inside of the vision of the qualified life and that your vision of the qualified life is the vision of our world today. Happiness, harmony, and so on. No suffering! That is a vision of life without any idea.

You have the last word.

Student: Initially, I thought that you were very generous to give me the last word. [laughter]

You've attacked me most on the point which is the weakest. That is, you've attacked me on the part on which I am least committed. I think that most of your attack hinges on a difference of the way we define suffering rather than a difference of the way that we define qualified life. What did you say, it was a very weak conception of qualified life? I do not think that our disagreement is about the relation between qualified life and suffering or about my weak conception of qualified life. Rather, I think you and I are using quite different conceptions of suffering. In a sense, this is of least importance to me. The thing that matters most is death as a concept.

I kept track. I'm going to skip over the first couple of things that you said about qualified life and come back to them if it becomes reasonable to do so. The main thing is that you equivocate in the way that you approach death. I think that it is a very important equivocation. On the one hand, of course I have an experience of death. Of course! It is true, and you're right. Of course I do. People pass away, and I identify with them. You said this to another student, it was part of your answer to her yesterday. We identify with people as they are passing away and we have this very strong and constant experience of death along a number of different axes. And of course, I have to agree. It is completely true, I would not argue with that at all. But ... what is interesting from my perspective does not concern the question of there being an opposition of life and death that is interesting for the question of how we constitute communities. We have to have ways of responding to the experience of loss that we name death, absolutely. That is good. Yesterday, you said that we would be uncivilized if we did not have this. We might have different ideas about what constitutes civilization, but I basically agree. I think that there is some necessity of symbolizing the experience of loss that we have hitherto called death.

My point is different. My point is that what we call death is a way of naming something that is radically uncertain. And it is radically uncertain precisely because the experience of identifying with somebody who is in the process of dying reaches its conclusion as an experience of identification at the point that we name death. Maybe before. It is true that there is a materialist commitment here, but I wouldn't call it empiricism. I want to say that when we are talking about the experience part of the objective/subjective binary ... I will come back to that in a moment. We want to talk about something that, materially, can occur. For instance, your example yesterday, and today again, was the novel. Do I think that I can not write a novel about something that I have no experience about? Yes, of course I can! But I can write a novel about something that I have no experience about because materially, from a fundamentally material …

Badiou: Just a moment. You said "I have no experience", but you must decide. "I have no personal experience because" …

Student: Wait, wait …

Badiou: … personal experience, I have … "I have no personal experience."

Student: I accept the amendment. That is, I think …

Badiou: It is an important point.

Student: Yes, it is a good point. One can write a novel about something one has no personal experience of precisely because the set of experiences that would define the world of the novel exist within the domain of materiality, broadly speaking. But the experience of dying, there is no such thing. Within where we are, nobody, that we know, has the experience of dying. Now, we actually do not know that nobody has experienced it either. I'm radically agnostic on this point. Absolutely agnostic. I have no idea whatsoever! For all I know, the Christians are right and the Mormons! There are three different kinds of heaven and you can visit between this kind and … I have no idea! The point for me is that this is the space of radical uncertainty. Interestingly, I have to say, I think, symptomatic of your stance in this disagreement …

Badiou: We have no idea uniquely because it is the end of subjectivity, so …

Student: Perhaps.

Badiou: We can not have an idea, but we have the idea that it is the death of subjectivity. It is sufficient! To be ...

[Badiou and the Student talk over one another for a moment]

Badiou: … to claim that something is the end is perfect knowledge of something. It is not the absence of the idea, it is precisely the idea! I search …

Student: But that itself is a belief that is not supported by anything but another set of beliefs. It is not axiomatic. So when you claim that death is the end of subjectivity, what we are left with is either we claim that it is the end of subjectivity or we can claim that it is not the end of subjectivity. Either I believe you or I do not believe you. Or, you can claim, as I do, that you are radically uncertain about what we want to signify. What would be the referent of …

Badiou: I do not understand your uncertainty. It is not an uncertainty. We perfectly know that death is the end of subjective historical existence. Maybe we can affirm that there is something after, and so on. But it is the end of the historical existence of the subject as such. It is perfectly clear. It is not uncertain! Because the question of the existence after death is an unhistorical question. It is the question of ...

Student: That is a tautology. It is only the case if, in fact, you are correct about what you are asserting. What I am saying is that we have no way of knowing. Take my example. It is a vulgar example. For example, assume that there is a small group of people living in the country side of Minnesota who do not know anybody outside of their little area. [Badiou attempts to interrupt the student, but the student continues] For them, it is absolutely the end of subjectivity to leave Minnesota. There is no subjectivity outside of Minnesota. And perhaps they are right.

Badiou: I claim that you maintain the religious hypothesis ...

Student: ... No, no no. [laughter]

Badiou: Yes! You maintain ...

Student: I maintain an uncertainty. That is precisely what the meaning of death would be; death as something that one takes on, assumes for oneself. Precisely, that is what remains in question. It remains in question in a such a way that does not allow itself being questioned within a dialectical worldview. That is my point. When you claim that I am maintaining the religious hypothesis, it would be true if I were saying that it *is* the case that what we experience as someone leaving the subjective community is not really so. That is the religious hypothesis. I do not affirm that at all. I have no opinion on it. I have no idea!

[Students begin interrupting one another]

Student: You are looking at it from the wrong direction. [laughter] When you claim that it is uncertain, you are one hundred percent correct. From one direction. And that is all you have ...

Student 2: ... and that is where you are beginning the religious hypothesis.

Student: No. It is where I am claiming that the question of what that direction means is not necessarily a religious question unless one insists on answering it. The second one answers ...

Student 3: ... it is the end, the end of subjectivity ... how you return from ... to the end ...

Student: This is circular logic. It is the end, therefore you can not ask about what happens after the end, therefore it is the end. That is circular logic. That is not a logic. If you say that it is the end therefore you can not ask about what it is.

Student 3: That is not what I said.

Badiou: In my opinion, death is our most certain conviction. There is no discussion possible. Nobody says, "oh! It is not death!" [General Laughter] It is true. It is something which is absolutely certain, death. There is no obscurity. There is no obscurity, except if you are within the religious question. It is the basis of something which is the very division of life itself between the moral part which is the body and the immortal part of life which is the soul. If you do not have this religious point then you have the certitude of death. Always.

Student: No. I think that by insisting on that binary you're maintaining a position – I will quote you here, "I think this vision is really inside the world" – to maintain that binary. The idea that there must be a certainty about what the signification of the term death is, is what I want to withdraw from. I do not want to offer a different signification. I am claiming that you insist that there is some point, in the sort of metonymic movement of signification, and that point is death. That all other significations are anchored to that point because we know what that point means is, for me, logically unsupportable. One can assert it, and I can not say "no, you are wrong, you must be wrong." My position does not allow me to say that. But it is logically insupportable. All you can do is point to experience. I have to say, here, you become an empiricist.

Badiou: I do not understand you, but you have the last word! [laughter] I can not understand it. For me, there is no obscurity about the fact of death. It is perfectly clear. There is no discussion, no division. There is only division if you are under some religious hypothesis. And so it is you who is religious and not me. The question of death is not at all a religious question. It is a historical question. Everybody must die. It is an absolute certainty. And so the question of the historical signification of this natural fact is our question.

I do not understand why we can not accept this. You are obliged to say that we can not have this position that there is no uncertainty concerning death as such. My problem is not the possibility of moral experimentation concerning death as such because I know perfectly that death is the end. There is no experience of death if experience signifies a personal and intimate experience. Death exists. That is the point. And it is precisely the relationship between death and the historical destiny of human beings which is my question. Not suffering. There is no relation between suffering and death. Suffering can be a loss of things, a historical adventure, suffering by illness, and so on. You can not substitute suffering to death. It is a completely different problem. You substitute suffering to death only because you maintain that death is a mystery.

Student: No, no. It is …

Badiou: We can not do anything concerning death …

Student: To maintain that death is a mystery is to affirm its continued value as a question. What I am claiming is that the question of the meaning of death or what would be signified by the term death …

Badiou: But it is perfectly clear! What you signify by the term death, it is perfectly clear … there is no question about this. It is a clear world.

Student: It is perfectly clear insofar as it is not dialectical.

Student 4: I think that where you are going is the question of birth. It is on the other side of death, and it is … [laughter] Yes, I mean. I am serious. I am not trying to cut in on your time, but death is what he just said. Death is what we can not experience. It exists but nobody can experience it. So what you are looking for is an answer to the question: what is the void? It is precisely this, that there is nothing. But there is something on the other side.

Student: What I am saying … Let me try again. I will say it very simply. I will try one more time.

Badiou: Ah! It is a good struggle! The living existence of death we find here today!

Student: What do we mean when we say the word death? What do we point to? Let us say that we use the word as a pointer of sorts. It points to something. It points to some set of differences. It refers in some way. It predicates. It signifies. We are pointing to the fact that, collectively, we experience members of the community of subjectivity ceasing to be radically and absolutely members of the community of subjectivity. On this I think we agree, absolutely. If anything can be named a fact then surely that can. So on this much, we agree.

My point is that to be a properly dialectical concept, to be a concept that is driven by an internal opposition in the Hegelian sense, death would have to not be something that admits of a perfectly clean and final cut answer. Without instantiating any religious hypothesis at all, it is enough to simply ask, and I think this is a reasonable thing to ask, on what logical grounds do we affirm that this collective experience is in fact the totality of what can be placed under the concept death? I would claim that we have no grounds for affirming that in any logical sense. We can affirm it empirically. I'm a materialist, I actually do not really believe in life after death. I am agnostic about all these things because I find that it does not harm me to be agnostic and it also does not seem to do any other larger harm. Really, very seriously, what we are naming, what we are saying, is an ineluctable fact. It is something that we agree on. And I am saying that something is precisely not an adequate content for the concept of death if death is to be a dialectical concept in its own internal being.

Badiou: You have the last word!

[applause]

Day Six

Seminar Ten

Classical logic * Existing is an immanent possibility of being * The identity function * First interruption: being and world * Second interruption: the body * What is an object? * What is a thing? * Neither Kantianism nor Pure Materialism * Third interruption: the subject * Fourth interruption: there is no time! * Regular change: change of existence * Singular change: event & truth

I propose that I try to completely explain the concepts of world, change, and event. Tomorrow we will read the poem by Valéry and I will answer the final question concerning the problem of ontology and change. So I will finish with a big part of the explanation concerning the question of change. That is our goal. If we do not finish today then we will return to it tomorrow. Okay?

I recall that a world is the localization of some multiplicities. This is a very small world:

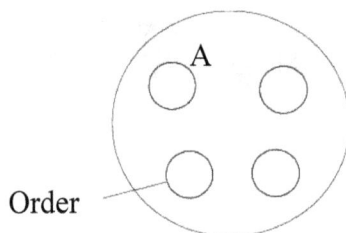

In general, we have an infinity of multiplicities. But we can not understand this question of infinity without invoking another question. So, I will return to this problem. The world is composed of a set of multiplicities and an order. Multiplicity *A* is a set which is inside of the world. The order is not outside of the world, it is inside of the world. This order has three fundamental properties: reflexivity, transitivity, and anti-symmetry. These three properties explain how it is possible that an order functions as a measure of identity and difference.

It is possible to organize the comparison between two different things. There can be a comparison between two different forms of identities or between an element and another element. We can also claim that this order has a maximum [*M*] and a minimum [*μ*]. From all of this we can explain why it is that two multiplicities, which are ontologically different, can also be be identical in a specific world. Philosophically, we can claim something like that. At the level of ontology there is a strict extensional principle of identity. It is the Aristotelian principle of identity. That is, *A* is *A*, *A* is equal to *A*. In a world, which is a particular localization of ontological multiplicities, we do not have this sort of principle of identity. We can claim that *A* is different from *A* in some sense, or, more generally, we can claim that the identity and differences can be absolutely different from the extensional law.

I recall that the extensional law claims that difference is always localized in one element. There is always one element that is in one multiplicity which is not in the other multiplicity. The difference is always something quantitative because the difference between two multiplicities resides in the fact that we can find something in one multiplicity which is not in the other multiplicity. So, the ontological identity is an identity of either "yes" or "no". In fact, the logic of being as such is a logic with only two values: either something is in the set or something is not in the set. This is of fundamental importance of identity and difference. We were in the world of logic then we could say, very simply, that the logic of ontology is equal to classical logic.

It is not the same thing when we are in a specific world. Maybe the logic of the world is classical. That is a possibility, but generally speaking it is not. There is no extensional definition of identity in a specific world. Rather, we have something like an intensive definition of identity; or, if you want, we have a qualitative conception of identity and difference. When the difference is qualitative then we can have many differences between the thing and the world which are not reducible to the classical difference. We can have a difference which is a small difference or a difference which is a big difference. At the ontological level, you are either identical or you are different, you can not have a big difference/identity or a small difference/identity. Everything here has no signification at the level of pure multiplicities. At the level of pure multiplicities we can only have the classical "yes" or "no", either you are identical or you are different. In a concrete world, this is not always the situation. We have a relationship of similitude whereby something is not exactly identical to something else but is nonetheless quite similar to something else. Something can resemble something else. There are many concrete variations of this, but we can not use classical logic to think about them.

In fact, it is the "yes" and "no" of ontology which is strange for us. In our common life we are within a world. We perfectly know that somebody is very similar to somebody else. I am identical to my brother, but not absolutely. We can experience a variation of all of this in the field of identity. Abstractly, some things are either identical or different, but it is not exactly true. It is only true if your logic is extensional and classical. If a point is different then it is absolutely different because all differences are absolute. But you actually experience something that is different but not radically strange. And so you experience something which is somewhere between identity and difference. All of this occurs when we are within the compromise of the world where an identity can not be as strong as that of the abstract level of ontological existence.

Okay, we can create some new definitions to explain how all of this works.

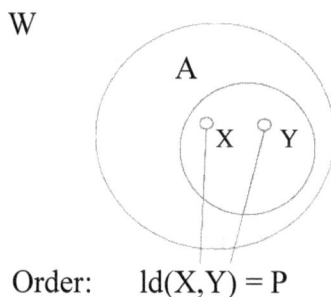

Order: ld(X,Y) = P

I have a world [*W*], an order, and a multiplicity *A*. *A* is in the world, it appears in the world. In the classical language of philosophy we can distinguish between *to be* and *to appear*. It is not in the sense that an appearance is something less existing than being because to appear is absolutely real. To appear is not an illusion, it is not a falsity. It is observable at the level of existence and not at the level of pure being. We can claim that being *A*, the pure multiplicity *A*, appears in the world *W*. It is interesting to say that the multiplicity *A* exists in the world *W*. It is much more useful and productive to not use the opposition between being and appearing – this is often interpreted in a Platonic sense – that is, to appear is something which is an illusion and is therefore not being. And so we should not maintain the clear opposition between *to be* and *to appear.* We must not claim that we must think being beyond all appearances. If you claim that *A* is a multiplicity, as a position in mathematics, and if you claim that *A* exists in the world, then we have a different position from the clear opposition between *to be* and *to appear.* Naturally, to exist is also *to be* because only something which *is* can appear. Only a multiplicity which is at the level of ontology is strictly being, but it can also appear. So it can exist. Existence is an immanent possibility of being. This is a very important point.

Existence is always relative to a particular world and a particular order. After that, we can claim that there are elements of the multiplicity named *X* and *Y.* I can not be too complex here, but these elements of multiplicities are also multiplicities because a "one" does not exist. A multiplicity is composed of multiplicities. We have affirmed that everything that *is* is a multiplicity. For example, a multiplicity is not composed of atoms, a multiplicity is not composed of pure unities. A multiplicity is composed of multiplicities. Very often, the pictures we use to represent this are not absolutely correct. In fact *X* is also something like that [Badiou points to *A* in the picture] but when they are elements of the multiplicity *A* they are conceived as elements of a multiplicity and not immediately as a multiplicity. In their being, they are multiplicities. The point is that if we do not accept the idea of a pure unity or a pure one then we must admit that all multiplicities are composed of multiplicities, and so on, until we must finally stop. And we stop with the void. We do not stop at the one, we stop at the anti-set. It is the set without any elements. It is fundamental to understand that elements in the set are something other than the set and yet, within the level of pure ontology, there are only sets. Elements of the set must be a set.

I will return to *A.* For *A* to be in the world there must be a value of internal differences of identities between the elements. We always have a function or an operation on the two elements of *W,* which is the identity function or the identity operation. The result of this function is an element of the order. The identity of *X* and *Y* is *P,* where *P* is an element of the order. Okay? All of this is a formulation of the very important idea that a measure exists for the identity between two things in a world. So *P* is only the measure of how *X* and *Y* are identical. If, from the point of view of the world, they really are identical, then the value of identity for *X* and *Y* is the maximum.

[Student interruption]

Student: But why are they identical to themselves? Like, I mean, why are they not in becoming?

Badiou: Why?

Student: Yes. Why are they not in becoming? Why do you presuppose that they are identical to themselves?

Badiou: Why do I presuppose what, exactly?

Student: … that they are identical. Why do you presuppose that you can say that two discrete elements are identical to themselves and that we can therefore make a relation between them. Why can't …

Badiou: No. We can take two different elements of the pure multiplicity. Ontologically, they are two different elements, no problem. When a multiplicity is in a world then all of the elements are in a world as well because a multiplicity is defined by its elements. If you put a multiplicity in a world then you naturally also put all the elements of the multiplicity in the world. It is the same thing.

Student: Right. I am taking the Deleuzian position that claims that there are no identities that can be compared. How can you get outside of that criticism?

Badiou: We must simultaneously be in the world and in ontology. This is always the point. We must think of the multiplicity as an ontological multiplicity. And that multiplicity is in the world. It is not a transformation of the former point when we move to the latter point. The multiple A is a multiple A at the level of being, and so all of the elements of the multiplicity A are also in the world. We can perfectly speak of two different elements at the ontological level which are measured concerning their identity at the existential level.

Naturally, your question is very good because we do not attempt to solve the question of change at the ontological level. But we can not solve the question of change at the pure level of the world. We must have the interaction of the two. The very strong idea here is that change is composed of something which does not change at the ontological level. The possibility of change will be the possibility of changing relations between a multiple and something else. For the moment we are only claiming that we are not inside of the change. In all of this, there is no thinking of the change. We are only thinking of change when a multiplicity is in a world and when we have an application of the function of identity on all of the elements of the set A. It is a pure fact concerning what it means to be in the world.

The fact is that to be in the world there is a measure of your identity. Okay? We can say: identity of X and Y is P. If, in this world, for this set, and for these two elements, there is a maximal identity of X and Y, then we can only claim that, from the point of view of the world, X and Y are the same. They are not the same at the ontological level. They are reduced to the same at the phenomenological level of the world. If the identity of X and Y, in a world, is the minimum, then we can claim that the identity of X and Y is something like zero from the point of view of the world. In a world, X and Y are absolutely different.

If P is neither maximal nor minimal then the value of identity depends upon the value of P between μ and M. It is very simple:

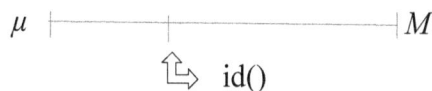

$$\mu \ \vdash\!\!\!-\!\!\!-\!\!\!+\!\!\!-\!\!\!-\!\!\vdash M$$

$$\Rightarrow \ \mathrm{id}()$$

Within the order of a world we have a minimum and a maximum and we can have many values which are intermediate. If we are within the classical world then we can only have two values. I recall that in a strictly extensional world, that is, within the ontological level, we have only two values because either the two things are identical or they are completely different. And so it is a value of minimum. Finally, we can claim that ontology is the level wherein the order contains only two possibilities: maximal identity or minimal identity, complete difference or complete identity. In general, this is not the case for our world here. We have many intermediate differences. Something is similar to another, something is not too different from another, a variant of red can be compared with another variant of red, the color red can be compared with blue, and so on. And so, in general, there are many intermediate possibilities of identity.

When two elements of a set are in a world the function of identity automatically fixes the value P for the identity of X and Y. P can be somewhere in between the minimum and the maximum, like it is in our picture. In the picture, the conclusion is that X and Y are not exactly identical but are also not completely different. When we are in a world we constantly have something like this – it is a question of experience. What is the difference between light blue and dark blue? You can not claim that they are the same color. It *is* blue, but one blue is lighter than the other, and so they are different. It is not possible to understand this point at the ontological level because we have only two value. As Parmenides claimed, either something *is* or something *is not*. Any problem, is this clear?

Student 2: Where does the body …

Badiou: Naturally, the body is inside the world. And maybe it is inside of several worlds.

Student 2: Okay.

Badiou: You know perfectly that your body is not absolutely identical to itself. In ten or twenty years my guess is that you will have the same body in some sense, and yet it will not at all be identical to itself. It is a good example because we must admit that something that we know at the level of being is also completely different in a concrete world. Perhaps you will not recognize yourself ten or fifty years later. In fact, everything which exists in a world is like that. It is like that because you can change your living body as an element of the world. It is a regular change.

Student 2: But there are also limitations.

Badiou: Naturally, there are limitations. There are some limitations because you can not become absolutely different. Very often, when we see somebody we have known, we will say: "oh, you have not changed! You are the same!" We are the same in one sense but different in another sense. From the point of view of your identity perhaps I can not recognize you. The difference between your identity at one moment and your identity at another moment may be very small. You must understand, however, that it is not too small – there is something here, for example. As a good friend you can claim "oh, you are the same." We are the same because we are not completely different. All of that composes the complete experience of everything that exists in a world. If this is clear then we can go on to give some definitions concerning the question of change.

First, we have a multiplicity, A, which is at the ontological level and which is absolutely identical to itself. Sometimes we have a world that is fundamentally an order plus multiplicities. We suppose that A is in W; A *"is in"* is not absolutely precise because *"is"* is not at this level. *"Is"* is at the level of ontology. We must say that it "appears" in the world or that it "exists" in the world. We can also claim that all of this concerns the localization of being. Immediately, we have the function of identity which operates on all the elements of A, and, you will recall, all the elements of A is A itself. There is something like a double determination. The pure being is submitted to the internal relation which measures the identity of two terms. So we can claim something very simple: at the ontological level there exists pure multiplicity and within a world there exists a multiplicity with the measure of identity. We can claim that we have A at the ontological level but we have A with an identity in a world. And the new identity is not the pure identity of the ontological level. In some sense, it goes from one to two. At the ontological level, A is completely determined by itself. That is, A is completely determined by all of the elements which compose it. This is the immanent definition of the multiple. It is a composition of the multiple by all of its elements. Once again, we also know that if one element is different then the entire set is different.

Things change at the level of the world. That which is in the world is defined by the multiplicity but with the new evaluation of identities inside the set by the order of the world. The world introduces the purity of being to a qualitative difference. In fact, it is an experience. When we are traveling to a new country it can be like a new beginning, it can be like traveling to a new world. It is a new beginning or a new existence. You can understand on what grounds I can assume that the measure of identities are different. At first we have the measure of our proper identity and we see that we are different in some sense. We are different because the world is not the same, not because we have changed. There is the question of language, customs, and so on. We are inside of all of that without knowing what constitutes the system of our identity with other multiplicities. To understand our presence in a world we have the feeling of ourselves as well as the minimal knowledge of the new order. The new order is that which organizes things in the new country. We know that we exist in a world when we pass from pure being to something else which is a measure of identity. The measure of identities is not the same in one world as it is in another world.

We do not speak about existence and we do not speak of pure multiplicity but we do speak of a multiplicity with a specific function of identity. We name an object this pairing of the two. You can speak of an object in a world. An object in the world is not reducible to a pure multiplicity. An object of the world certainly is a multiplicity but with something new which is the internal measure of identity of elements of the set by the new order of the world. And, finally, we have the elements of A. The elements of A are submitted to the function of the measure of their identity. We name an element of an object a thing. And so we have an element, an object, and a thing.

You know, a thing is nothing else but an element of an object which, in turn, is a multiplicity with a function of identity between its elements. A thing is what is submitted to the operation of identity between elements. When we have A in a world we also have a measure of all of the elements of A. We can claim that an object is a being which appears in a world and all of the elements of this object are things by the measure of the order concerning their identity. This brings us to an old philosophical question concerning the difference between being and object. In general, is there any difference between an object and being? It is the first very important philosophical discussion.

For example, in Kant we can find the idea that an object is completely different from being. True being can not be known as an object. An object is something that occurs from the subjective point of view in relation to our perception of the world. It is an elementary point. We have a philosophical decision. The organization of the relationship between being and object for Kant was distinguished between the ontological level and the level of the world but only through a complete separation. An object was not at all a true presence of being, it was not real being because we do not know real being at all. And so it is the first question: what is the difference between an object and being or what is the identity between the object and being.

We can claim that for pure materialism the object and being are the same thing. There is no difference between the mysterious being behind the appearances and the appearances of objects. This is why the materialists offered the first critique of Kant. Marx, Engels, Lenin, and all of the modern materialists were critical of Kant first of all because of Kant's opposition of being and object. An object is a subjective creation of our understanding and being is something we can not know, being is mysterious. Pure materialism reduces being to the object. There is an object here, and there is nothing else in than the objects of the world.

You know, my proposition is to have neither one position nor the other position. I do not admit Kant's critical vision because we can know pure being or pure multiplicity. There is a science of pure multiplicity which is called mathematics. We can not completely know pure multiplicity because mathematics is rich with discovery, but we can know something about pure being. There are new mathematical discoveries every day. Being as such is present in the object. The object is being as such in a world and submitted to an order. I do not agree with ordinary mathematicians because I think that we can not reduce being as such to objects. Objects are always objects of the world and so we must admit that it is not exactly the same thing as *to be* as such. To be in the world is to be localized and submitted to an order. The complete conception of all of this is necessary for us to have a new understanding of change. The idea of change is very different if you are within the Kantian conception or within the conception of the pure materialists. It is why I had to explain all of that to you.

In philosophy there have been two great discussions about the signification of the word "thing". Why is "thing" different from "object"? Can any of you say a word about the difference between an object and a thing?

Student 3: Is an object something that always relates to a subject? Is a thing something that …

Badiou: So we can not have any perception of a thing.

Student 3: A thing could be a subject or an object.

Badiou: A thing could be a subject or an object? So your definition is that an object is opposed to a subject?

Student 3: … related to a subject.

Badiou: … related to a subject but different from a subject. And the thing is anything which exists. Subject and object.

Student 3: No. A thing is always something material. So it couldn't be anything that exists.

Badiou: And you do not admit that there are mountains?

[student interrupts conversation about things]

Student: But how does temporality come into this? Quentin Meillassoux discusses time with a capital "T". I'm just wondering where his ideas would fit into your description of objects within a world.

[short silence]

Badiou: Yes, yes. Finally, you know, you can have the first proposition. Your first proposition is to say that an object is something which is opposed to the subject. It is different from the subject and in relation to the subject. So objectivity is something which is in some relation to the subject. I have another question for you. In your vision, an object is something different from a subject but in relation to a subject, but what is this relation?

Student 3: Well it could be the same. An object and the subject could be the same. What is the relation between the object and the subject? It could be the same.

Badiou: Between an object and a subject? Yes – you have said that an object is in some relation to a subject and the thing is outside of this relation. Or something similar. But what exactly is the relationship between subject and object?

Student 3: What is the relationship between subject and object?

Badiou: Yes, because you said that at the beginning.

Student 3: Um, that is a very difficult question.

Badiou: You know, your position is Kantian by necessity because if you put an object on one side and the subject on the other side then the object can not be defined like it is here. An object, here, is only *to be* in the world. There is no difference between object and subject. It is only *to be* a multiplicity in a world. To be a multiplicity in a world is not to be in a relation to the difference between objects and subjects. If you claim that the object, and finally objectivity, is by necessity in a relationship to a subject then you are within the vision that claims that objectivity depends on subjectivity. And so it is the Kantian vision.

It is possible that you are within the Kantian vision. It is not a crime! But, to clarify the problem, the thing must be material. Is that how you have said it? The thing is material. If this thing is material then we have to claim that something exists which is not material. Everything which exists is a thing. A thing would be what exists in a world. In this case, the difference between object and subject comes after the level of the thing. Everything that exists is a thing and after that we have the difference between subject and object. You know, this is why the distinction between object and thing has been really difficult. If you are within the Kantian vision then you must first distinguish between subjectivity and objectivity. And subjectivity is constitutive of objectivity. But if you admit that there exists something like a thing then the thing must be the abolition of the difference between subject and object because a subject in the end must also be a thing.

What is a thing? It has been a very difficult question. We can not place the notion of a thing when we have a distinction between subjectivity and objectivity. Do you understand? It is the title of the famous text from Heidegger: What is a thing? In Heidegger's text there is a conception of being which is not at all my conception of being. His conception of being includes a very acute discussion of the thing. A thing must be a product of the temptation to do away with the materialist vision of being. Generally, the word "thing" is something like a materialist word. I agree with you. It is because everything which exists is a thing. You know, all of this is a part of a very difficult set of problems from philosophy. But in my own construction, it is all very clear [laughter].

We have the perfect vision of the distinction between being, object, and thing. No? The question of the subject becomes complex [laughter]. So, you can put all of the complexity onto what is completely absent here today, and that is the notion of the subject. If you want to say something concerning objectivity which is not Kantian, which is not the reality of the subject, then it is reasonable to have no subject at all in the beginning. After that I introduce a notion of subject and subjectivity. But if you have subjectivity at the beginning then you are within the Kantian vision: the dependency of objectivity to subjectivity.

To recapitulate, we have the ontological level of being and an object which is a pure multiplicity inside of a world. Finally, we have the thing which is the element of an object. Okay. An element of an object is relative to a world. To have a thing we must first of all have an object in the world and an element of the object submitted to the order of the world. If to exist is to be submitted to the order of the world then what properly exists is a thing. With any object we have the function of identity, but the function of identity prescribes the identity of elements of the set. What exists in a world is always a thing. Or, if you want, the world is composed of things. In fact, it is composed of sets. But, as a world, what is important, is the thing submitted to the order. Finally, if a set is submitted to the order of identity then it is because its elements are submitted to the order. It is because a set is nothing else, and so we can say that a world is composed of things.

A thing is not determinate. The thing is not determinate but the object is determinate. A thing is everything. We must recall that a world is composed of things and that this is a materialist point of view. Things are always in a set, the thing is a component of an object. The object is in the world with the function of identity. If we transfer all of that at the elementary level then we can claim something like: to be in a world, to exist in a world, is to exist somewhere in the world. We do not exist at the absolute generality of the world. We know that. We always exist somewhere in the world. Naturally, it is the case that an element of an object exists somewhere in the world because the object is precisely somewhere. We can change the world. We can be more empirical. We have the world, W, and we have the order of the world. We can say that two multiplicities appear in the world. This signifies that the elements of the multiplicities are immediately submitted to the law of identity. We can claim that the thing – the element or the thing – is in the world, is at the place of the world. You are somewhere in the world when you are a thing.

We can say A for X and Y is their site or their modality of presence in the world. It is where they exist. It is something like my family or my country.

[student interruption]

Student: Can you talk about how time fits into your ontology? There is this relation, of course, but what about temporality? What about becoming? How does it work?

Badiou: Well … what?

Student: Time!

Badiou: No. For the moment there is no time! [laughter]

[audience laughter]

Student: For the moment? No time? Really?

Badiou: Time is something else. We must construct time.

Student: Really? So, you're a Kantian then …

Badiou: We can not begin by time. If we begin with time then we have no understanding of anything. It is the difficulty of the Heraclitian position. The Heraclitian position begins with time, begins with change, begins with becoming. But if we begin with becoming then we can not say anything about what composes becoming as such. That will always be the difficulty concerning the question of time. If we begin with change then we can not have a true understanding of change because you identify change and being. My attempt is to give the entire theory of change its Parmenidean part, the part of non-change which is a necessity to understand change. And I return to science. To completely understand movement, Galileo, the creator of modern physics, happened by necessity to claim that a movement is always relative to something which is not in movement. We can not have a general and indistinct movement. It is non-intelligible.

By this construction we can understand change. It is our goal. And so we go toward that goal. For the moment we only have the general conceptual disposition of the different components of change: being, object, and thing. Now, we can have the question: what is a change? What is a change in a world? And for understanding what a change is in the world, we must have in mind the other question: what is a thing? When we have a complete understanding of what a thing is then we have the question concerning the changing of a thing. This is now our question.

We must first recall that the existence of the thing is the identity of the thing to itself:

$$Ex = id(x,x) = p$$

Why do we say the word existence? It is because we know that we can not have a change of being. Being as such can not change. And so if something changes then it is by necessity existence which changes. The existence of a thing, which is naturally an object, is the relationship to itself by the function of identity. I recall that the identity of x and x has some value which is somewhere between the minimal and the maximal. We must affirm that if a change exists in a world then this change is by necessity the change of the existence of some thing. The change at this level is in some sense existential. The change is existential. By its very nature it is a change of existence.

Why can the existence of the thing change? How is it possible? The thing can not be in different objects. This is why the existence of the thing can change. You know, there is no necessity in a world: x can be an element of object A but it can also be an element of another set. In pure being we can have two different sets with some of the same elements. There is certainly in B an element which is not in A but the difference is always point by point.

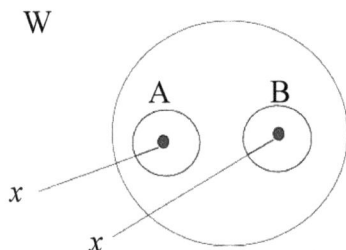

It is not at all possible that an element is in two different places. The change is possible because the place where the thing is can be different. So a change is always when something exists between A and B. This implies a sort of transferring of x from A onto B.

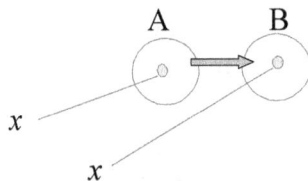

It is when we transport ourselves from a place to another place. That is a change. If we consider ourselves as a thing to examine then: you come from a completely different country and you can be in another completely different country without completely changing the world but by changing your place in the world. You were a thing in France or in Switzerland and you are not a thing in Turkey or China. All of this assumes that we consider China as an object of the global world. It is also possible for you to be a thing in Switzerland and also a thing in China. But all of your differences inside the first are not by necessity in the second because the second also has a function of identity. The function of identity is not the same in a different country of the world. Maybe it is the same, but probably it is not. It depends on our concrete experience of the difference between China and Switzerland. The measure of a thing in China can be compared to a thing in Switzerland. Maybe the differences are submitted to the same law in China as in Switzerland. Maybe, in Switzerland, you are almost identical to many others and maybe in China you are almost different from many others. You understand, there is a very simple understanding of change.

Change concerns displacement in a world. It is impossible for a thing to appear in different places. Maybe the difference is in time, because perhaps the composition of the world includes A and B but not simultaneously. Perhaps B comes into the world after A, and x is transferred from A. So we can construct a complete theory of time from that. I do not know ... you can do it [Badiou points at the first disruptive **student**]. Change is always a movement but it is a qualitative change because it is absolutely possible that the value – it is generally the case – of existence of x ...

$$(Ex)A \qquad (Ex)B$$

If we name the existence of x like that [(Ex)], then the value of the existence of x is in A. We have the value of existence of the same case in B. There is no reason that the value is the same. The context of the evaluation of identity is not the same. The relationship between them – the thing x in the object A – is not by necessity identical in the context of B. And so we have a change of existence. The change of existence is, in fact, a change of object. The thing is transferred from an object to another object and it can transform the self-identity of the thing, and so it is possible to have a change of the thing.

When I claim that the thing changes, I really mean that there is a change of the existence of the thing. Behind that, there is something invariant because it is a multiple. It is the same multiple with another existence. You know, this was precisely our starting problem concerning the understanding of change. If something is absolutely changed then you can not understand the idea of the change of something. The change of something is only interpretable if you can identify the thing which changed. In the case here, we have a change of the complete existence of the thing. The thing is a being but its being is the same.

So, we can say that we have being, object, and thing:

$$Being \quad A \quad {}^{\#/} \quad B$$

$$\uparrow \qquad \uparrow$$

$$Object \quad A \qquad B$$

$$\uparrow \qquad \uparrow$$

$$Thing \quad x \implies x$$

$$(Ex)A \implies (Ex)B$$

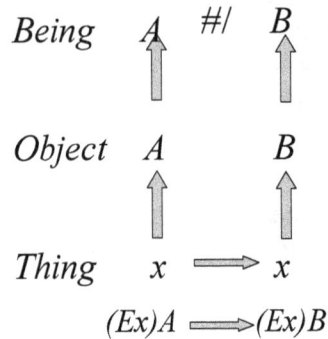

Being, object, and thing. The thing changes its existence from A to B. The existential change of the thing is the difference of two objects. The difference of two objects is ontological because A really is different from B at the ontological level. We have two different beings at the ontological level and these two different beings are inside the same world. The beginning of the possibility for change is that two different beings are in the same world. There are in fact in the same world and x was an element of A and was always an element of B. So x becomes a thing in the world but a thing in different possible places. It is a thing in object A but also a thing in object B.

The possibility of two different existences in the same world is the basis for the possibility of change and it is also the basis for the understanding of time. It provides us with an understanding of the correlation between space and time. This is always the question. From the very beginning the understanding of time is linked with the understanding of space. Quite frankly, we have space/time – the dialectics between space and time. In fact, the understanding of relativity is a difficult problem. Philosophically, we can claim that we have solved the interaction between space and time from the point of view of change. Change implies an ontological difference, a difference of being, and not only a difference at the level of perception.

You know, that sort of change can not imply a change in the world. The possibility of that sort of change derives from the fact that the thing, x, can be in different objects. If you have objects with the same thing then you have the possibility of a change of existence from the thing. But the thing is inscribed in the world itself. It is not a change of the world. This is why I name this change, regular change. It is a simple modification of the value of existence. A regular change is a contextual change. It is a change inside of the objective laws of the world. To change is to be in another place and to change a place is also a change of objectivity or a change of the value of existence. This is a change of the value of identity. And the change of place can also be a change of places in time.

When we claim that the world is composed of objects we have no idea about this composition. The composition can be of many sorts. To completely understand the different possibilities of the compositions we must employ more technical and more complex means. But you understand that the world is composed of objects, that objects are composed of things, and that all of this correlates to an order. It is a very simple explanation.

We can explain what a change is in a world, abstractly. It is not a concrete explanation. The change must be in time and space. We must distinguish space from a world. The world is a composition of multiplicity with some order. We must be satisfied with a clear answer to our essential question: how is it possible to have change without having the complete dissolution of the thing? We can understand in what sense our change is the change of nothing. A thing is determined at the ontological level but the existence of the thing is submitted to change. Sometimes accepting change means that it must be possible for the thing to have a great and perhaps maximal value of existence in an object of the world. After some change the value of the existence of the thing might become minimal. This is the abstract definition of death. It is the becoming of value zero within existence. Death is the degree zero of existence in a particular world. We have returned once more to death!

Do you understand the movement? We can name death the process of change which goes from the positive value of existence to the minimal value of existence. It is the possibility for the thing to disappear; being in the world, but with the value zero of existence. All of this concerns regular change. All of this concerns changes inside of the laws of the world. You know, the condition of regular change is the presence of a thing in different places; that is, the condition of regular change is the presence of a thing in different objects. But when we interpret the empirical world of an object and thing, there is some difficulty.

We have the framework to understand that the same thing can change its value of existence. The real question is: is there a change which is not a regular change? If a change is not regular change then it is a chance which is not the passage to another localization of the thing, to another object. The substructure of the change is the presence in the same thing in different objects. The condition of regular change is the possibility of the presence of the same thing in different objects. So, a change which is not regular is not a change which is the consequence of the presence of the thing in different objects but is a change which affects the object itself. It is the change of the place of the thing. It is when one natural place in the world, when an object in the world, is, by itself, the support of the change.

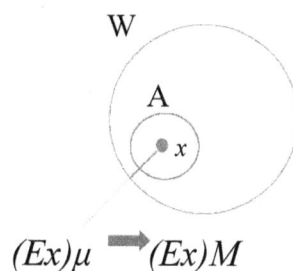

$$(Ex)\mu \implies (Ex)M$$

A change is a change of the object and not of the thing of the object. That is the point. Something is transforming the law of identity itself, in this case. It is not the change, or a place, but rather it is a change of the identity function itself from the same object. Suppose that in the same object, x – not by the change to another object – we have a change of the existence of x. For example, maybe we have moved from the minimum to the maximum. Suppose for the moment that something like that has happened. We have no explanation. It is impossible. It is impossible because the existence of x in A is fixed by the order and the identity function. In this case, we have a change of a completely different nature. It is a change of the relationship between the object and the order. The value of x in the beginning is not the same as the value of x at the end.

Normally, the value of x can not change. The object is A and it has a function of identity. The object, which is composed of a fixed function of identity, assigns strict values to every element. Okay? If we have a change inside the same object then it is because something real happens. It is not deducible to the laws of the world. If something happens in this form, that is, if something happens between the multiple of the thing and the identity, then we can speak of singular change. How can something like that happen? How can something like that happen without any external determination? We only have A and B, and A is a function concerning every x which are elements of A. We must begin to understand singular change.

We must assume that all of this happens inside and that there are no external elements. It is by necessity that something happens to the function of identity itself.

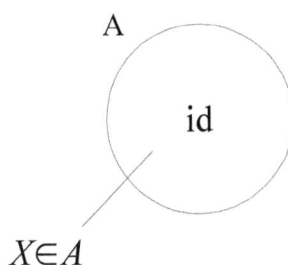

My proposition derives from the psychoanalysis of many events. My understanding is that there is a sort of movement of being as such to appear by itself. I imagine it to be something like a volcano. Generally a volcano is quiet. But inside of the volcano, by definition, there is an internal being of the volcano, the cause of the volcano, which sometimes goes toward the surface and appears. An eruption of a volcano occurs when something which was inside goes outside. I claim that the strength of being as such appears at the surface of the world itself but from the internal composition of the world.

The fact is that the object falls under the identity function and not only the thing. The object wants an identity. The object, which is behind everything which appears and behind the law of the world, has something like a strength toward the direction of appearing. At the surface of the world there is a sort of non-distinction between being and object. There is a moment when an object becomes a thing. Recall that a thing is an element of A. If the object falls under an identity then it goes that way because what happened was something like an object appearing by itself. There is a violence on the part of ontology for appearing, in the appearance of being as such. Naturally, this is why an event has a relationship with truth.

There is a relationship between event and truth. In an event, there is the appearing of being as such. We have something like the becoming thing of being. It is why I provided the image of the volcano. A singular change occurs when we have something like this phenomenon, which is the appearing at the surface of the world of the profound being. In the world, the profound being is always here. But it is not always visible because what is visible for us is only the measure of identity and difference; qualitative identity and qualitative difference. What is visible? This object is blue, and so on. There is an infinite of identities and differences in the qualitative sense and all of this composes the experience of the world. There is a sort of invisibility constitutive of being which is the truth of that which does not exist. We can remark that an object does not exist because to exist you must have some value of identity. Or, we can remark that the object has no value – only the elements of the object or of the set has value. We can say that being in general does not exist.

A good metaphor is the Marxist conception of the proletariat. The proletariat is certainly the fundamental truth of society because it is the productive class. It is the class that produces everything that exists. But, in the organization of society, they are invisible. They do not appear as what they are. Precisely, they do not appear as the true being of society. And what is revolution? A revolution is the becoming visible and dominant of the truth of society, which is the class and the great majority of the people. All of this is included in the abstract vision I have outlined here. When we have a sort of eruption of being at the surface of the world, that is, when being as such takes a point of existence in the world, then we have something like the following:

$$\mathrm{id}(A,x)$$

… the identity between an object and a thing. We can read this as: inside of the object there is an identity of the object and some thing of the object. For singular change, it is the becoming of an equality between thing and object.

And that is the most profound conception of an event. I name all of that an event. An event is precisely when we have the becoming thing of an object in a world. That is, an event is when we have a complete change of place in the hierarchy. It is a complete change of identity and the visibility of being as such. This is the most interesting definition of an event. It is when we have an equality between the level of objectivity and the level of thing.

Do you know about the great music of the workers? "We are nothing," the Internationale. "We are nothing, now let's be all!" It is precisely the same thing. We are only things, we must become objects. Objectivity is one of being inside the world for being. Maybe a thing is a modality of existence of something in the world. At the end of our trajectory today, we can claim that an event is when we can not distinguish between being and necessity, being and existence. Generally, being does not exist. Naturally, an event is not something ordinary. An event happens. In some sense it happens beyond the law of the world because it is precisely the existence of pure being.

A truth is something which touches the real in a world. A truth says something which is not completely relative to the world but which is universal. It touches something of being. There is a close relationship between truth and event. An event is the eruption of being in the field of existence and not in the field of particularity of a world. To go beyond the particularity of the world we must have something indistinct between being and existence. And so it is clear that an event is always the condition for a truth. The condition for a new truth is the condition for a new movement from the particular to the universal or the generic.

But the event is not by itself a truth. I must return to this point. An event is the opening of the possibility of a truth. It is the opening of the possibility of creating something which is beyond the particularity of the world. A truth is inside the world like a work of art, an exceptional poem, a scientific invention, or a political revolution. A truth involves concrete men and women acting toward something which is beyond the particularity of the world and which can be understood from the point of view of another world. And, why? It is because a truth is something which is in a relationship to being and not only to the relative function of identity. To understand something like that we must have an event at the very beginning. We must have something which happens and which is the sudden convergence of existence and being. And that is a singular change.

[extended applause]

Seminar Eleven

What is truth? * From being to truth * The subject in the dimension of its affects * Passion for the real * The problem of urgency * What is a subject? * Subjectivation * Beyond anxiety, to courage * No creation without anxiety * The Graveyard by the Sea

Thank you for being here today. It is an unofficial day, not a regular day. And so, in some sense, you are not obliged to be here. It is by perfect freedom that you are here. Very good. I will divide the final discussion into two parts. First, I will answer three questions which as a group are very different. I will explain why they are different momentarily. After that, I will provide a reflection concerning one possible reading of Valéry's poem. Both of these parts are unified by the last possible question concerning change. Finally, the last question is not a question for today. It is a question which comes after the solution of the question of change. It is the question of the subject.

Why is it a question of the subject? It is because the subject appears under the condition of an event. To approach the question of the subject we must first have an understanding of an event. More generally, we must have an understanding of a change. We can organize all of this into a very simple picture:

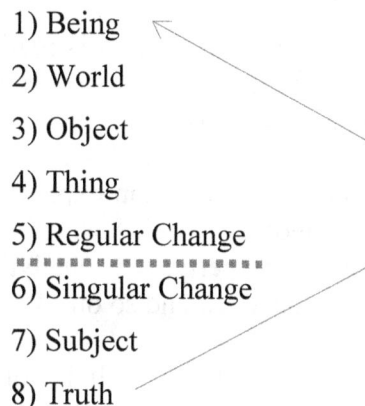

1) Being
2) World
3) Object
4) Thing
5) Regular Change
••••••••••••••••••••
6) Singular Change
7) Subject
8) Truth

First, we have the level of being. Second, we have the possible existence of the world. Third, we have the level of the object. Fourth, the level of the thing. Fifth, the possibility of regular change. I recall that regular change is a change of a thing from the point of view of a different object. After that there can be something different, a singular change. Seventh, we have the level of the subject. A possible happening of something new inside of the world under the condition of singular change takes the form of the subject. A subject is always singular in some sense, it is not reducible to human animals. Human animals – you and me – exist at the level of things. And we are interesting things [laughter]. The becoming subject of a human animal is always under the condition of singular change. This is why the subject is separate from a thing, it concerns the question of singular change.

At the final level we have another complex problem. The eighth level is the level of truth. The level of truth has a relationship to the first level of being. Truth is something which is always in a world. It is an important point. Truth is not outside of the world because a truth is something produced in the world by the action of a subject under the condition of an event or singular change. Truth, as a production in a world, is not reducible to the law of the world because there is a singular event between the law of the world and the object of the truth. We are in a world but not exactly under the law of the first world where all of this happens. This is the first characteristic. The second characteristic concerns something which is inside of existence and says something concerning being. A truth is in some sense the possible existence of being, or, more precisely, a truth concerns a form of existence. A truth exists, it is a form of existence in which something is said concerning the presence of being in a world. It says something about the presence of being in a world but not only in the form of existence but also in the hidden form of its pure presence. If being appears in the world then it does not appear as such, it appears as an object. A truth is something which exists, and for something to exist it must be inside.

A truth has a relationship to the negation of an event because an event is something like a circumstantial appearance of being at the level of existence. You know, a truth is something which exists, but inside of its existence there is also something not reducible to the laws of existence. There is something which is first of all inside of the laws of existence but it is also not reducible to the productive capacity of the laws of existence. There is a similar event which has a relationship not only with existence but also with truth as such. Naturally, this is why we can claim that a truth is eternal. What is the signification of the word eternal? It means: having a value for many worlds, and maybe it means having a value for all worlds.

The possibility of a truth having a value for many worlds is really obscure because there is no world of all worlds. When we are speaking about all worlds we are really speaking about something which is unclear. Certainly, a truth is something that can have an existential value in some other world in relation to the world wherein the truth has been constituted. This is why it is common to claim that truth is universal. It is a common expression to say that the truth exists first in a world and has an existence in another world. I will finish this point by claiming that universality is not reducible to a formal property. The analytical definition of universality concerns universal judgment: for all x you have …, and so on.

First, truth is creation. There is an objectivity to truth. It is something which is created in a specific world. Second, truth is the result of a process of construction. Third, truth implies the subject. Finally, it is the global generic result because it is a generic object. It is the result of the process of a generic object which can be understood as universal existence in some other world rather than the primitive world where the truth has been created. This is the signification of the eternity of truth. It is not the value of truth because the existence of truth is not reducible to one world. You can create an English name for this if you like. Maybe it can be something like trans-world. It must be more interesting than the word universal because the word universal is too formal and it is opposed to particularity. When we have a pure universality, it seems that there is something obscurely oppressing about it because it is something imposed on particularity from the outside. This is why we sometimes claim that universality is imperialist in nature, that it is imposed onto other cultures, and so on.

This is not the case concerning the question of truth. Truth is only a possible proposition of the existence of other worlds. There is nothing imposed. It is simply the possibility of a value of truth in another world. We can turn to plays from Sophocles. Sophocles was in a very obscure world. He was not in our world at all. I do not claim that we must impose Sophocles onto everybody. It is only a possibility or a proposition. It is a proposition of a truth. At this level it is also possible to understand the existential and formal value of the geometry of Heraclitus. It is a proposition for our world and not something imposed onto us by Greek magistracy.

We have the complete representation, the complete picture, of the first movement from being to truth. You can see that truth is not at all the intuition of being or a new relationship to being, but rather it is the production of something in a world. It is the production of something which depends on a world, object, thing, regular change, singular change, subject, and so it is a picture of the first movement from being to truth. It is not a necessary movement because we can not find the causality of a truth in being. Being can not explain a world, being can not explain a singular change, and being can not explain a subject. But there is a trajectory from being to truth with something like a change. There is a truth by change because singular change is not a necessity. It is also a picture of some return to being. The truth is being from the point of view of what happens in a world.

The group of three questions are very different precisely because they are more complex. They are questions concerning the subject. I propose that you read the three questions and then I will discuss the common point from all three of them. So I can not give detailed answers to the three questions. I can give you a global message. Will you begin?

Student: In *Logics of Worlds* you made the important claim that an evental truth subject is a subject that breaks with repetition and enters into a new affective relation to the trace of the idea. The way that I understand it is to claim that the only affect that can create the universal conditions for the evental body is the affect of anxiety. This ushers in an event precisely because it is that affect that has no object. This is what makes the event universal. Do you agree?

For example, for the subject that rejects the truth, as well as the obscure subject, the event is still universal and felt because of the anxiety that the universal event ushers in. We know that the primary affects of an evental truth subject are joy, happiness, pleasure, and enthusiasm. We can affirm the creation of a new human in relation to the idea. We know that for Lacan, repetition precedes repression because the real is a minimal difference and repetition is what establishes the symbolic order. Are you proposing that desire precedes castration for the evental truth subject? Do you accept the comparison of the evental truth subject to the project of Deleuze and Nietzsche as a kind of overman? In essence, an evental truth subject is above self-reflection. We understand that your debate with Slavoj Zizek is primarily around the Lacanian real. However, in what way does the real become repositioned in the world of an evental truth subject? In what way does the real become positivized?

In the unfolding of evental namings and nominations, and engaging of the traces of the truth exposed to a world, you have spoken about logical arrogance around determining the intensity of an in-existent within a world. What is the relationship between logical arrogance and foreseeing? Is there an ethical question or project to be done between the idea of foreseeing and logical arrogance?

Finally, in what location are we to locate the unary trait in the eruption of an event? In what I understand, for the event, the master signifier is replaced by what you call the unary trait. Is the unary trait that which extinguishes the master signifier? Can a post-evental body operate without a master signifier situated to a world?

Badiou: To punctuate this question: a complete answer to all of the questions you have asked would need a second complete session of six days. Maybe we can do something like that next year. It is impossible to do this immediately. I just want to say that one of the most important questions relates to the subject in the dimension of its affects. The question concerns the subject when it is confronted by the event and the consequences of the event. It is by necessity always approached by that sort of situation.

Student 2 This is a shorter question. Your first lecture was on ecology. It is safe to assume that we have a limited amount of time to establish a new vision of the relationship between history and nature, human and animal, and so on. You have said this. How does this necessity of urgency shape your politics? Is it not now, more than ever, that a passionate absolute change is needed? If I can qualify this … I know that, as far as I understand, within your philosophy there is no absolute change because change is always localized. Again, what I am trying to get at is this urgency. Maybe one of the typical criticisms of your philosophy is that it leads to a Messianism, a waiting for the event.

Badiou: Alright. You know, I agree with the claim that the ecological question today is a subjective question much more than an objective question. At the objective level we know the facts, practically. The conclusion is that we must do something. We must absolutely do something. In the end, doing something is a subjective determination at the level of government, private citizens, organizations, and so on. But we must do something. Your question is about urgency and passion. It is now more than ever that a passion for absolute change is needed … a passion for absolute change.

It is interesting because the passion for absolute change was the revolutionary passion of the last century. The consequences of this passion have met difficulties. I propose that the passion for the real was the passion of the last century. The passion for the real was the passion to create a new world. What you want is the absolute passion of the subject. In some sense, it was the passion of the subject for a singular event. It was not the idea that the subject was under the condition of an event, rather it was the typically Leninist idea that change is under the condition of a new subject. The position was that an event is always a subjective production. Naturally, if an event is a subjective production then there are not subjective elements. When the subject is a consequence of an event there is something which has an internal limitation of the possibility of the subject because the subject depends on the consequences of the event. If the subject is the pure creation of the event itself, in the form of an absolute political revolution, then we know that there is an infinite possibility and an infinite subjectivity; a subjectivity that would infinitely create.

Terror is a consequence of this vision. It is the vision of the omnipotence of the subject. The subject might be the party, it might be Stalin himself – there are many incarnations. Philosophically, we can understand the relationship between event and subject. Here, we have the subject as the god or master of history because he is able to create absolute change. After a century of the passion for the real we must have something different. We must have something which is not the passion of the potency of subjectivity. This position is the constant glorification of the subject.

More precisely, we must have a consideration of the responsibility of the subject concerning the organization of the consequence of the event. This position is more cautious. I think that it has been said by Foucault and others: this vision is a vision inside the question of the death of god. This vision claims that human beings are the new god. It is humanity as such that is able to become the master of history, the new historical god. So there is a creation by something presented as a subject which affirms its own infinite power. It affirms its infinite power insofar as it affirms itself as the master of history. If we accept the more moderate claim that the subject is the space of the consequences of an event and not the master of the event then you do not have an infinite power. And it is not possible to have, as a consequence, a terrorist state. A terrorist state can not be created. The man, the activist, and the party, was created through a large appropriation of many millions of people and under the idea of a new form of historical creativity. The position was something like a substitution of the classical transcendent god of the religious vision by a human god, or humanity itself as god, inside of history and with all of the infinite powers of god.

What is the problem with destruction? If we have an infinite potency to create then we can destroy. After all, it is a small part of infinity. If you kill millions of people then you know that death is the destiny of everybody. So we destroy before something natural happens. If you are the master of history and if you have the infinite power of history then you have the conviction that destruction and death are tactically necessary. This was the position of all of the activists of the last century. Violence, and finally death, are a tactical necessity because we have the possibility of an infinite subject. That is my explanation concerning the point of urgency.

To claim urgency is to claim that we must do something. But are we the master of nature? It is not exactly the question of the relationship between history and nature. Are we the master of nature? Probably not. Our actions are very much against nature. Nature is something infinitely bigger than our action. We can not repeat, for ecological reasons, the same representation of the subject as we have found in political activism. You question is not inside the question of nature but it is at the level of the question of the subject. In some sense everybody knows that we must do something and that there is a possibility that we all know the reasonable thing to do. Today, when somebody says "no, it is not necessary to do something important," it is because this person does not trust himself. It is a question of private interests. We must do something but not just anything. When I am dead we can do something. For the moment it is not an imperative. To others "yes," but me? "No."

It is not really a question concerning knowledge. We can find a real consensus concerning what we must do. But, what is a subject for these processes? Government? Public opinion? Science? What, precisely, is a subject? What is the common measure between this possible subject and the possible natural event in the global field of ecology? It is why I believe that the true question of ecology is not a question concerning the knowledge of risk, nature, destroying parts of nature, and so on. These questions are clear. The real question is more obscure. It is the question of the subject who is in charge of finding the solution to the problem.

You know, it is striking that you returned to the question concerning the passion for absolute change. This is what I find most interesting in your question. Because you – not you, but your sentence … is similar to the position of a Bolshevik ecologist [laughter]. It is very typical. A Bolshevik ecologist has an urgency to find a solution. You must do something. What is the subjective feeling? An impatience for absolute change. It is a passion for absolute change which necessitates the destructive passion. For example, this can include the destruction of the enemies of ecology: reactionary governments, anybody who are opposed to what must be done. These are real problems. The passion to do something is the passion to become the master of the problem, by necessity, and it is the Bolshevik solution. By what means? International meetings? Scientific deliberations?

Your call for urgency for a sort of subject that has the passion for absolute change but, you know, in the end not all things have the passion for absolute change. It is an operation of absolute conviction.

The third question … she is not here? I call this question "the mystery of being". In fact, it is not a question. It is a sort of declaration concerning the different forms of subjectivity in relation to being as such. It is interesting because it is representative of a mystical formulation. The mystical orientation claims that you have a direct connection between being and truth. The subject is constantly defined by its direct correlation between truth and being. Truth is precisely the direct intuition of being as such. The mystery of being is also the mystery of the subject and the subject is in a state of fusion with being.

My global answer would be that we certainly have a question of the subject at the level of subjective affects. Why? It is because you must go beyond your pure ordinary life in order to participate in the consequences of an event, you must orient your existence in a world in the direction of a singular change. Naturally, your ordinary life is composed of regular change. It is possible to define living in a world as the existence of regular change.

If we have a singular change then it is different. First, human animals are not obliged to go in the direction of singular change. Precisely, regular change is the law of the world. Singular change provokes the individual with something like a choice to go in a direction which is against the ordinary direction of the world itself. This is subjectivation, the subjectivation of the individual, the subjectivation to accept and be interesting in the consequences of something like a new truth. What is interesting is to go from existence to being, it is the possibility to use a truth to say something concerning the presence of being in a world. Certainly, the subject has this sort of position after an event. There is something like a passion for being which is not distinguishable from the passion for truth.

We can have some passion, some affect, which is not the ordinary affect. Ordinary affects are linked to regular change. But when we are in the logic of singular change affects exist which are not affects of existence but of the relationship between existence and being. The ecological orientation is something like that, in some sense. Your passion for absolute change is a passion for a relationship between the historicity of human beings and something which is on the side of nature. And so it is true that there is something like anxiety.

Why anxiety? There is something like anxiety because we must know something that we do not know. There is a part of the real that we know exists but we do not really know what it is. This is also the case for an event. There is an opening of new possibilities. What is the realization of these possibilities? We do not know. We simply know it point by point during the very difficult process of the construction of a truth. We know it piece by piece, but at the beginning we do not really know anything. But it is not the absence of knowledge about something about which we have no idea. It is an appetite for knowledge about something which is precisely our choice. It is our choice to be engaged with something which is not immediately clear to us. It is a promise.

An event is something like a promise of something new. It is a promise of something which is not reducible to the ordinary laws of the world. What is the world with this novelty? It is not immediately clear. Maybe, after the novelty, the world will be terrible or absolutely obscure and confusing. We do not know. Maybe the novelty will destroy life. Maybe. So, anxiety is constitutive of the creative subject. There is no creation without anxiety. And there are different forms of anxiety. In some sense, this is a matter for psychology, but there is always anxiety. If we have anxiety then we must always have the dialectical means to go beyond anxiety because anxiety by itself is a negative affect.

In fact, I agree with Lacan on this point. I believe that anxiety is a thing for a new real, for a real we do not know. Lacan claimed that anxiety is too much real. That is, anxiety is a real which is not the real that we know. Rather, it is a real which is something like an excess of real. From the beginning, the promise of a new real is by necessity also something like an excess of real. It is the promise of a real which is beyond the real. If the true affect of anxiety is something like the impossibility to act or the impossibility to do something then it is pure anxiety. I will stay in my bed. To stay in your bed is not a creative position. It is contrary to the choice to go with the consequences of an event in the direction of something new. The affect of the human animal in this circumstance is anxiety, it means that you are afraid and you retreat to the old world. This is very often the case.

Many humans decide for a moment to go in the direction of the new possibility but they are inevitably interrupted by anxiety. We must also have an affect which goes against anxiety, and this affect is courage. Courage gives the human animal the means to go beyond anxiety. There is a dialectical relationship between courage and anxiety and it is at the very core of the construction of the new subjectivity. In some sense, anxiety is a necessity to indicate to the subject that there really is something new in the situation. Anxiety is something like a new subjective knowledge of the situation and courage is the affect that goes against anxiety in the direction which exists by the anxiety itself. Anxiety claims "oh, there is something new! And it is terrible!" Courage claims, "I will go in this direction, I will go beyond anxiety!" So, there is a dialectical relationship between anxiety and courage. Only when anxiety exists can the therapy for anxiety provide us with courage.

This is the general law. The subject, at the level of the personal affect of the human animal, is composed of a dialectics between anxiety and courage. I have experienced this personally. After all, I also have a body. It was during the sequence just after May 1968. The collective situation was obscure and confusing. We had the consciousness of something absolutely new but it was not representable or visible. There was a lot of subjective anxiety. It was not an anxiety relating to a fear of the enemies. Not at all. It was an anxiety concerning the new as such because the new is always obscure and this obscurity is the real. Our choice was to do something, and we did many things. But doing something was always within the context of subjective anxiety because the promise of the situation was really obscure. Simultaneously we did many things which were completely new – we spoke with people we did not know, we visited workers in factories, we invented new languages, we had late night discussions, and so on. We were very tired. We didn't sleep. We were unclear with anxiety. But we continued, we decided to continue. It was a very strong and concrete experience. At the beginning, it was really the experience of the event as such. After all of that, you know, we experienced some failures. But the beginning was really a complete subjective mixture of the dialectics between anxiety and courage.

To conclude on this point I will claim that the question of the subject always occurs between the question of singular change and truth. For many reasons, I can not completely explain all of this. It is linked to infinity for many reasons, because a truth is never complete. A truth must always be completed by something else. When a truth is in another world it is always because the truth will be completed by a new aspect in this other world. The universality of truth is also the positive continuation of truth. It is not a pure passive reception, it is a continuation.

This is perfectly clear in the field of the work of art. The work of art is not a passive reception of truth, it is a continuation of something. It is the process of doing something the same way but which is nonetheless different. It is also perfectly clear in the political field. What are the lessons of old revolutions? What is the lesson of the Bolshevik revolution? The lesson is, in some sense, to something completely different but in the same way. So it is to continue the truth. This is a very important point. The universality of truth is an active universality rather than a passive universality. If something is universal for you it is because you can continue the truth as universal, as a generic set. But the subject is always the subject of the creation of truth between the singular change and the truth in a concrete situation.

In some sense, the subject is between time and eternity. The subject is between the most radical form of change, which is singular change, and the most radical form of eternity, which is truth. The subject is the active term between the change in the world and the non-change of being. This is why there is a mixture between anxiety and courage. There is an uncertainty of the dialectics between change and radical change as a result of something like a magnificent peace; the eternal peace of being.

This was also the concrete feeling I had in my experience. Anxiety and courage were linked together. We were in fidelity to an event. The goal of the struggle was not exactly change as such but rather a new peace, a new eternity, and a new form of human beings as such, outside of the anxiety and disorder. It is a personal image of the situation between singular change and truth. The subjectivity of creation in all fields – the political one, naturally, but also artistic and scientific change – and also the vision of a new theory and a new world involves a definition of a new peace. No? This is the dream of the scientific field. In some sense, we must have the courage to continue this position because singular change is finished. Singular change happens and then it is finished. But truth does not finish, it is eternal.

We are in a very strange position. It is the creative position of human subjectivity between something like a radical change, which is finished, and something like a true eternity, which is something unfinished. We are neither in absolute change nor in absolute non-change. We are between the two. And it can not be a peaceful subjectivity. It can not involve harmony or pure happiness, and so on. It can not be something like that. Rather, it must be something more complex like a divided subjectivity between the part of anxiety and the part of courage, but also between the part of knowledge and the part of uncertain action, and the part of time and the part of eternity.

Now I will give you a few words concerning the poem.

The Graveyard by the Sea
Paul Valéry (C. Day Lewis, Trans.)

This quiet roof, where dove-sails saunter by,
Between the pines, the tombs, throbs visibly.
Impartial noon patterns the sea in flame –
That sea forever starting and re-starting.
When thought has had its hour, oh how rewarding
Are the long vistas of celestial calm!
What grace of light, what pure toil goes to form
The manifold diamond of the elusive foam!
What peace I feel begotten at that source!
When sunlight rests upon a profound sea,
Time's air is sparkling, dream is certainty –
Pure artifice both of an eternal Cause.

Sure treasure, simple shrine to intelligence,
Palpable calm, visible reticence,
Proud-lidded water, Eye wherein there wells
Under a film of fire such depth of sleep –
O silence! . . . Mansion in my soul, you slope
Of gold, roof of a myriad golden tiles.

Temple of time, within a brief sigh bounded,
To this rare height inured I climb, surrounded
By the horizons of a sea-girt eye.
And, like my supreme offering to the gods,
That peaceful coruscation only breeds
A loftier indifference on the sky.

Even as a fruit's absorbed in the enjoying,

Even as within the mouth its body dying
Changes into delight through dissolution,
So to my melted soul the heavens declare
All bounds transfigured into a boundless air,
And I breathe now my future's emanation.

Beautiful heaven, true heaven, look how I change!
After such arrogance, after so much strange
Idleness – strange, yet full of potency –
I am all open to these shining spaces;
Over the homes of the dead my shadow passes,
Ghosting along – a ghost subduing me.
My soul laid bare to your midsummer fire,
O just, impartial light whom I admire,

Whose arms are merciless, you have I stayed
And give back, pure, to your original place.
Look at yourself . . . But to give light implies
No less a somber moiety of shade.

Oh, for myself alone, mine, deep within
At the heart's quick, the poem's fount, between
The void and its pure issue, I beseech
The intimations of my secret power.
O bitter, dark, and echoing reservoir
Speaking of depths always beyond my reach.

But know you – feigning prisoner of the boughs,
Gulf which cats up their slender prison-bars,
Secret which dazzles though mine eyes are closed –
What body drags me to its lingering end,
What mind draws it to this bone-peopled ground?
A star broods there on all that I have lost.

Closed, hallowed, full of insubstantial fire,
Morsel of earth to heaven's light given o'er –
This plot, ruled by its flambeaux, pleases me –
A place all gold, stone, and dark wood, where shudders
So much marble above so many shadows:
And on my tombs, asleep, the faithful sea.

Keep off the idolaters, bright watch-dog, while –
A solitary with the shepherd's smile –
I pasture long my sheep, my mysteries,
My snow-white flock of undisturbed graves!
Drive far away from here the careful doves,

The vain daydreams, the angels' questioning eyes!

Now present here, the future takes its time.
The brittle insect scrapes at the dry loam;
All is burnt up, used up, drawn up in air
To some ineffably rarefied solution . . .
Life is enlarged, drunk with annihilation,
And bitterness is sweet, and the spirit clear.

The dead lie easy, hidden in earth where they
Are warmed and have their mysteries burnt away.
Motionless noon, noon aloft in the blue
Broods on itself – a self-sufficient theme.
O rounded dome and perfect diadem,

I am what's changing secretly in you.

I am the only medium for your fears.
My penitence, my doubts, my baulked desires –
These are the flaw within your diamond pride . . .
But in their heavy night, cumbered with marble,
Under the roots of trees a shadow people
Has slowly now come over to your side.
To an impervious nothingness they're thinned,
For the red clay has swallowed the white kind;
Into the flowers that gift of life has passed.
Where are the dead? – their homely turns of speech,
The personal grace, the soul informing each?
Grubs thread their way where tears were once composed.

The bird-sharp cries of girls whom love is
teasing, The eyes, the teeth, the eyelids moistly
closing, The pretty breast that gambles with the
flame, The crimson blood shining when lips are
yielded, The last gift, and the fingers that would
shield it – All go to earth, go back into the game.

And you, great soul, is there yet hope in you
To find some dream without the lying hue
That gold or wave offers to fleshly eyes?
Will you be singing still when you're thin air?
All perishes. A thing of flesh and pore
Am I. Divine impatience also dies.

Lean immortality, all crêpe and gold,

Laurelled consoler frightening to behold,
Death is a womb, a mother's breast, you feign
The fine illusion, oh the pious trick!
Who does not know them, and is not made sick
That empty skull, that everlasting grin?

Ancestors deep down there, O derelict heads
Whom such a weight of spaded earth o'erspreads,
Who are the earth, in whom our steps are lost,
The real flesh-eater, worm unanswerable
Is not for you that sleep under the table:
Life is his meat, and I am still his host.

'Love,' shall we call him? 'Hatred of self,' maybe?
His secret tooth is so intimate with me
That any name would suit him well enough,
Enough that he can see, will, daydream, touch –
My flesh delights him, even upon my couch
I live but as a morsel of his life.

Zeno, Zeno, cruel philosopher Zeno,
Have you then pierced me with your feathered arrow
That hums and flies, yet does not fly! The sounding
Shaft gives me life, the arrow kills. Oh, sun! –
Oh, what a tortoise-shadow to outrun
My soul, Achilles' giant stride left standing!

No, no! Arise! The future years unfold.
Shatter, O body, meditation's mould!
And, O my breast, drink in the wind's reviving!
A freshness, exhalation of the sea,
Restores my soul . . . Salt-breathing potency!
Let's run at the waves and be hurled back to living!

Yes, mighty sea with such wild frenzies gifted
(The panther skin and the rent chlamys), sifted
All over with sun-images that glisten,
Creature supreme, drunk on your own blue flesh,
Who in a tumult like the deepest hush
Bite at your sequin-glittering tail – yes, listen!

The wind is rising! . . . We must try to live!
The huge air opens and shuts my book: the wave
Dares to explode out of the rocks in reeking
Spray. Fly away, my sun-bewildered pages!

Break, waves! Break up with your rejoicing surges
This quiet roof where sails like doves were pecking.

[end]

Why this poem? We can find in the poem an explanation of being, world, object, thing, regular change, singular change, subject and truth. It interesting for me because of its poetic presentation.

The beginning of the poem is the presentation of a place which is a symbol of a representation of being before change. The poetic names for this representation of being as such are, principally, three. First, the sea. The sea is presented as a potency of pure repetition. Second, the sun. The sun is the absolute immobility of light. Finally, there is the interplay between the sun and the sea. And so it is not at all three concepts [laughter]. It is not at all the old maxim of the disorder of life. There is absolute order between the sea and the sun. It is because the sea is presented as something like a mirror of the sun. There is either an identical relationship between the sun and the sea, and the subject, which is the poem, is absorbed by all of that. The author is fascinated by this vision.

The third term is death. Once more, we are confronted by death. It is death because there is a cemetery at the level of the sea. We have the idea that dying, to be dead, is adequate to being; death is a part of being. We see at the end of the poem that it is not a part of existence, but it is a part of being. The poem says somewhere that the death is on the side of the complex unity between the sea and the sun. The description of death in the poem is something like an ontological discussion of the passage of something which exists to something which *is*. Death is the part of infinity and immobility. It is not at all the idea of the soul. There is an explicit critique of the traditional vision of the theory of the soul at the very end of the poem.

The first part of the poem is a long and subtle discussion. There is a complicity between the sun, the sea, and death. And this complicity between the sun, the sea, and death is a sort of temptation for the subject/poet. The temptation is to go in this direction and to abolish his consciousness. We can see that this is something like a world. It has some objects, for example the sea and the sun. It has some details, plans, and memories. But it is a world which includes a temptation to be in the world of being and not the world of existence. For all of that, the word is absence. It is a world where everything is realized in the form of a general absence of life and not in the form of the presence of life. The poem is a temptation for the subject to be, to vanish, to disappear in some sense. It is exemplary that at the very end of this long-winded discussion of the world of being, everything which is important is in the details. Naturally, I will reduce all of this to the abstract form.

At the end of the poem we have Parmenides. The poet mentioned the cruel philosopher Zeno. The poet claimed that his own subjective situation is something like being killed by the philosophy of Parmenides. The poem moves from the appearance of a world to a pure vision of being but not in the sense of singular change. The first big part of the poem seems to go in the reverse: from the appearance of change in the sun, sea, and landscape, progressively toward a sort of potency of death and a new form of fascination of immobility. And, finally, at the final reduction of all of that to the philosophy of Parmenides, it moves to the Parmenidean vision which is the absolute primacy of being unchanged.

Brutally, we have here a rupture. We have the intervention of a completely new object which is not here. It is the wind. The sun is dead, but we have the wind. With the wind, which is the image and violence of singular change, the poet wrote that we must try to live. We must try to live. If the world is only the world of being then finally the world is the world of death. All of this is in conformity with Parmenidean philosophy. There is no change, the real, the truth, is the absence of change. Brutally, there is a rupture, which is an event inside of the world. It is the refusal of all of that in the name of change. The metaphorical presence of change is the wind. The wind is coming so we must try to live, but to try to like means taking the consequences of the wind; that is, it means taking the consequences of what is not reducible to the complicity between the sun, the sea, and death.

After that, we have details and images. It is a splendid poem. It is not reducible to philosophical speech. When we have in mind philosophical speech you have a new interpretation of the poem. The poem is not only about the glory of change – this is most apparent at the end of the poem. The poet claims, at the end of the poem, that we must be in the world of life. It is Nietzschean, if you like; life against death, and so on. But the most important point of the poem concerns the temptation of death. It is the temptation to be Parmenidean. The temptation is, in some sense, a mystical temptation. It is the temptation to disappear into the global world of immobility. The temptation for the poetic subject is to be inside the glorious and splendid images of the world of death.

Finally, there are some moments in the poem that describe death as a critique of being. But what is a critique of being? A critique of being is absurdity. There is a real temptation to claim that the true signification of life is death, the true signification of the appearance of change is being without change. We go toward the Parmenidean philosophy. The poem brings us to the point of refusing Parmenides and toward an opening of something which is immediately Heraclitian in nature. The movement of the sea itself changes. The sea becomes the new sea of the movement of change. After the Parmenidean world there is the beginning of the Heraclitian world, and this latter world claims that there is a truth to life. The truth of being in a world amounts to the opportunity to live, because the change of being is the change of death.

You know, it is a change of death only because we are not within the complete movement of everything. There is an opposition of the direct relation to being, which is a temptation of mystical experience and it is very near the experience of Messianism, and the acceptance of regular change. This is why we can conclude with the poem and state: I want to say thank you all, really. It is not always in the past. Really, it is a pleasure to speak to you. So thank you.

[extended applause]

Other books available from Atropos Press

5 Milton Stories (For the Witty, Wise and Worldly Child), Sofia Fasos Korahais

Beautiful Laceration, Gina Rae Foster

Che Guevara and the Economic Debate in Cuba, Luiz Bernardo Pericás

Grey Ecology, Paul Virilio

heart, speech, this, Gina Rae Foster

Follow Us or Die, Vincent W.J., van Gerven Oei

Just Living: Philosophy in Artificial Life. Collected Works Volume 1, Wolfgang Schirmacher

Laughter, Henri Bergson

Pessoa, The Metaphysical Courier, Judith Balso

Philosophical Essays: from Ancient Creed to Technological Man, Hans Jonas

Philosophy of Culture, Schopenhauer and Tradition, Wolfgang Schirmacher

Talking Cheddo: Teaching Hard Kushitic Truths Liberating PanAfrikanism,
    Menkowra Manga Clem Marshall

Teletheory, Gregory L. Ulmer

The Tupperware Blitzkrieg, Anthony Metivier

Vilém Flusser's Brazilian Vampyroteuthis Infernalis, Vilém Flusser